I dedicate this book to all of my horses, past and present: Pretty Chant, Can Can, George, Hotspur (Laddie), Zazie, Dusty, Big Jake.

Title: GREAT *HORSEWOMEN OF THE 19TH CENTURY IN THE CIRCUS* *and an Epilogue on Four Contemporary Écuyeres: Catherine Durand Henriquet, Eloise Schwarz King, Géraldine Katharina Knie, and Katja Schumann Binder*

Copyright © 2015 by Xenophon Press LLC

ISBN: ISBN: 9780933316621

ebook ISBN: 9780933316638

Copyright © 2001 by Hilda Nelson as *The Ecuyere of the Nineteenth Century in the Circus with an Epilogue on Four Contemporary Ecuyeres,* 2001

Previous ISBN 0933316143

Illustrations in Chapter X courtesy of Mme. Catherine Durand Henriquet, Ms. Eloise Schwarz King, Circus Knie, and Big Apple Circus / Theo O. Krath.

All rights reserved. No part of this work may be reproduced or transmitted in any form or by any means, electronic or mechanical, including photocopying, or by any information storage or retrieval system except by a written permission from the publisher.

Published by Xenophon Press LLC

7518 Bayside Road, Franktown, Virginia 23354-2106, U.S.A.

XenophonPress@gmail.com

Cover image: Blanche Allarty-Molier performing the Capriole on d'Artagnan.

THE GREAT HORSEWOMEN OF THE 19TH CENTURY IN THE CIRCUS

And an Epilogue
on Four Contemporary Écuyeres:
Catherine Durand Henriquet,
Eloise Schwarz King,
Géraldine Katharina Knie,
and
Katja Schumann Binder

by HILDA NELSON

With a Foreword by DOMINIQUE JANDO

© Hilda Nelson 2001
© Xenophon Press 2001
© Xenophon Press 2015

Xenophon Press Library

Xenophon Press continues to bring new works to print in the English language whether they be new works, such as this one, or translations of older works. Xenophon Press is dedicated to the preservation of classical equestrian literature.

Available at www.XenophonPress.com

30 Years with Master Nuno Oliveira, Michel Henriquet 2011
A Rider's Survival from Tyranny, Charles de Kunffy 2012
Another Horsemanship, Jean-Claude Racinet, 1994
Art of the Lusitano, Yglesias de Oliveira, 2012
Austrian Art of Riding, Poscharnigg 2015
Baucher and His School, General Decarpentry 2011
Dressage in the French Tradition, Dom Diogo de Bragança 2011
École de Cavalerie Part II, François Robichon de la Guérinière 1992
Equine Osteopathy: What the Horses Have Told Me, Giniaux 2014
François Baucher: The Man and His Method, Baucher/Nelson, 2013
From Destrier to Danseur, Tucker/Mistral 2015
Great Horsewomen of the 19th Century in the Circus, Nelson 2014
Gymnastic Exercises for Horses Volume II, Eleanor Russell 2013
H. Dv. 12 Cavalry Manual of Horsemanship, Reinhold 2014
Healing Hands, Dominique Giniaux, DVM 1998
Horse Training: Outdoors and High School, Etienne Beudant 2014
Legacy of Master Nuno Oliveira, Stephanie Millham 2013
Methodical Dressage of the Riding Horse, Faverot de Kerbrech 2010
Racinet Explains Baucher, Jean-Claude Racinet 1997
The Art of Traditional Dressage, Volume I DVD, de Kunffy 2013
The Ethics and Passions of Dressage Expanded Ed., de Kunffy 2013
The Gymnasium of the Horse, Gustav Steinbrecht 2011
The Italian Tradition of Equestrian Art, Tomassini 2014
The Maneige Royal, Antoine de Pluvinel 2010
The Manege Moderne, D'Eisenberg 2014
The Portuguese School of Equestrian Art, de Oliveira/da Costa, 2012
The Science and Art of Riding with Lightness, Stodulka 2014
The Spanish Riding School & Piaffe and Passage, Decarpentry 2013
Total Horsemanship, Jean-Claude Racinet 1999
Wisdom of Master Nuno Oliveira, Antoine de Coux 2012

Available at www.XenophonPress.com

TABLE OF CONTENTS

Publisher's Preface vii
Acknowledgements ix
Foreword xi

Chapter I 1
    A Brief History of the Circus and the Franconi Dynasty

Chapter II 16
    The Horse is King in the Circus

Chapter III 27
    The *Ecuyère* is Queen in the Circus

Chapter IV 38
    Women and Sports

Chapter V 44
    Caroline Loyo, Pauline Cuzent, Antoinette Cuzent-Lejars,
    and the Cuzent / Lejars Company

Chapter VI 67
    Madame Marie Isabelle and the École de Cavalerie of Saumur

Chapter VII 85
    Anna Fillis, Elise Petzold, Emilie Loisset and Elvira Guerra

Chapter VIII 105
    Comtesse Fanny Ghyga, Baronesse Jenny de Rhaden

Chapter IX 120
    Adèle Drouin, Diane Dupont, Blanche Allary-Molier and
    Marguerite Dudley

Chapter X 135
    Epilogue: Catherine Durand Henriquet, Eloise Schwarz King,
    Géraldine Katharina Knie, and Katja Schumann Binder

Glossary 165

Bibliography 169

About this book 173

Index 177

PUBLISHER'S PREFACE

It is with great satisfaction that we are able to bring back into print, Hilda Nelon's masterwork, *The Ecuyere of the Nineteenth Century in the Circus with an Epilogue on Four Contemporary Ecuyeres,* 2001. On first glance, many readers of the origianlly titled work may not have known what an *"Ecuyere"* is or was. Hence, I realized that the title ought to be in English in order to apeal to a wider audience. The true heroines of the 19th century circus were indeed the lady riders. Hilda Nelson's mission of bringing the culture and exploits and accomplishments of these great equestrians to light was somewhat thwarted by an unecessarily obscure title. Now available worldwide both as a print volume and as an e-book, This text can now reach a much wider audience.

It is very clear that Mrs. Nelson was inspired both by the *equestriennes* of the 19th century and the four *equestriennes* of the 20th century. In turn, we hope that the illumination of the culture, life and times of the great horsewomen described in this volume informs, enlightens and inspires generations of equestrians.

—Richard F. Williams
Editor-in-Chief
Xenophon Press LLC

ACKNOWLEDGEMENTS

I wish to thank the following persons and institutions for their help in assembling this book:

Claude Chauvineau, Bibliothèque Gaston Paris, Université Paris III, for helping me locate the books on the circus that are part of the Pierre Féret Collection.

Celine Bodving, Hors les murs, Centre des Ressources, who, in an E-Mail message, put me on the right track with respect to circus information.

Erin Foley, Archivist, and Bernice Zimmer, Library Assistant, Circus World Museum, Baraboo, Wisconsin, for making available to me the catalogue of the Robert L. Parkinson Library and Research Center and for sending me so promptly the books needed for my work.

Michel and Catherine Henriquet of Le Fief de la Pannetière, Autouillet, for their hospitality and generous time they spent with me when I visited them to interview Catherine with respect to the Epilogue.

The Inter-library Loan Departments of San Diego State University and the University of California, Santa Barbara, for locating and sending me the books requested from the R. Toole-Stott collection on the circus.

Pascal Jacob, Christian William, and Madame Bonvallet for their hospitality at Panem et Circenses and placing at my disposal their collection of books on the circus.

Dominique Jando, Associate Artistic Director of the New York Big Apple Circus, the first person to put me on the right track for suggesting the many books I should read on the history of the circus, for mentioning the libraries and bookshops I should visit in Paris, and for sending me photocopies from the books in his private collection. Above all I wish to thank him for reading the manuscript for accuracy on the history of the circus and his copious annotations.

Chris Krenger and Pascale Giger, the Press Office of Cirkus Knie, for their hospitality when I visited Cirkus Knie in October during its sojourn in Lausanne. They provided me with information, photographs, and articles on Geraldine Knie, her family, and Cirkus Knie. I also wish to thank Chris Krenger for providing me with tickets and a seat to the circus, despite the fact that on some occasions performances had sold out.

Matthias Van Halst, Centre de Documentation et d'Archives du Cirque, for sending me an email message concerning a bibliography of books on the circus.

I would also like to thank my publisher, Xenophon Press for believing in this work and for reprinting it in the second edition for the benefit of another generation of readers.

Last but not least, I wish to thank my husband, Burt, for taking care of chores during my absences in Paris and Lausanne, and during the time spent in my study, and for reading the final manuscript, noting spelling and typographical errors, and making several suggestions.

FOREWORD

To most Americans the word 'circus' often carries unsavory connotations. The circus is mostly seen as a rather chaotic traveling spectacle, which, as a form of entertainment, can be put in the same category as carnivals, freak shows and other lowbrow types of amusement. For over a century, speaking of the circus as a performing art in this country has been perceived as a rather daring, if not simply bizarre, approach. Fortunately with the arrival on the old American sawdust and spangle scene of such successful circus art houses as the Big Apple Circus, Cirque du Soleil and, most recently, Barnum's Kaleidoscope, this negative perception has finally been slowly shifting—at least in the urban centers visited by these upscale traveling circuses.

Circus is seen differently in Europe—than it was in America in the late eighteenth and early nineteenth centuries, when circus performances were presented in amphitheaters especially built for the presentation of equestrian displays in the circus, or ring, and to which were added acrobatic exhibitions, clowns (the eccentric actor and acrobat inherited from the Elizabethan theater) and pantomimes— grandiose (or advertised as such) spectacles that mixed drama, clowning, acrobatics and horsemanship. New York alone saw fifteen of these amphitheaters, or circus buildings, come and go from 1793 to 1870. (The last one was the Hippotheatron at Union Square and Fourteenth Street, then at the heart of the theater district.) Yet by the 1830's the American circus had changed drastically. It had become a huge commercial success. It appealed to all classes of society, yet was especially attractive to an ever growing population of immigrants who were not always at ease with the English language and therefore particularly enjoyed the largely visual form of entertainment the circus offered. Consequently the American circus attracted business entrepreneurs who took the place of the old artists/managers, and put the show under canvas to travel more easily and reach an ever spreading population. Thus the traveling circus became the American norm, and its transitory status (here today, gone tomorrow) drew in its wake a population not always reputable. Circus tents grew larger (longer, that is, since it was technically the only way then to make them effectively bigger) to accommodate an increasing number of customers. And more rings were added to allow these customers to see a slice of the show, even if they were seated at the very end of the newly elongated tents. By the turn of the twentieth century, up to seven acts could perform simultaneously under an American Big Top. Under such conditions, artistry quickly gave way to mere spectacle. Altogether, the American circus lost its soul.

At the same time in Europe, the traveling circus was mostly considered ersatz, only good for the consumption of remote villages and country towns. To see the real thing, you had to go to the city, where world class artists performed in the splendor and comfort of the local circus buildings—which were often as luxuriously appointed as the best local theaters or opera houses. There, equestrians, acrobats and clowns performed for a knowledgeable audience who could appreciate all the subtleties of their craft. Great circus dynasties were not seen as mere traveling entertainers: although they indeed originated in that often decried category, the Schumanns belonged to Copenhagen and Stockholm (and Albert Schumann to Berlin); the Carres to Amsterdam; Ernst Renz was a Berliner; Geromino Medrano, although a Spaniard, and the Italian Franconis were Parisian; Ciniselli was a household name in Saint Petersburg (notwithstanding the fact that Gaetanno Ciniselli was Italian); the Austrian Albert Salamonsky reigned over Moscow's circus; and the very British Price family were part of Madrid's cultural life. Great international acts traveled from one of these major circuses to another; and it should be noted that, at their level, one didn't mingle with the lesser performers who peopled the traveling circuses.

Circus was quite a serious thing in nineteenth-and early twentieth-century Europe. Edmond and Jules de Goncourt noted in their Journal 'We go to only one theater—the Circus. There we see clowns, tumblers, men who jump through paper hoops, all following their profession, all doing their duty, in reality the only actors whose talent is incontestably as absolute as mathematics or, better still, as a somersault. For in that, there is no false exhibition of talent; either one falls or one does not fall.' Balzac believed that a circus equestrienne was worth more respect than an actress, a prima ballerina or an opera prima donna. And indeed, equestrians were the kings of the circus—and equestriennes, its idolized queens. For horsemanship was important then. It was more than mere entertainment. Wars had been won by good horsemen. Horses still were man's most valuable partner in so many aspects of every day life. And the circus had been created by and for equestrians.

So let's forget the perverted image we might have acquired of the circus. Hilda Nelson takes us to a wonderful, often surprising journey with the greatest circus equestriennes of the nineteenth century, who reigned with so much flair over the most prestigious rings of Europe. These are stories generally known only to circus scholars, and rarely told to the public at large, especially in America. Ms. Nelson spent a great amount of time with these grandes *ecuyères*, researching their saga in libraries here and in Europe. She puts back the spotlight on these unjustly forgotten stars of the circus of yore. Circus buffs, as well as horse lovers, should be grateful to her!

—Dominique Jando

> *Au cirque plus qu'alleurs, la lutte pour la vie fut souvent la course à la mort.* (Henri Thétard)
>
> In the circus, more than elsewhere, the struggle for life was often a race towards death.

CHAPTER I:
A BRIEF HISTORY OF THE CIRCUS AND THE FRANCONI DYNASTY

Humans have always had the desire to be entertained, no matter how poor or how simple their society, and no matter how informal the entertainment. Thus, a precursor of the circus, as it was eventually established in the eighteenth century, and not necessarily under a roof, has always existed. Whenever wandering jugglers, acrobats, rope dancers, or trainers of animals appeared in a village, at fairs, at the gates of a city or a castle, people gathered, curious, wanting to be entertained.

Ancient documents reveal that Egypt and China presented various types of spectacles in a ring, which could be called a circus. In fact, a hippodrome was established by the Pharos for chariot racing. There is evidence that acrobatics on horseback were also performed. According to Monica J. Renevey in *Le Grand Livre du Cirque,* the murals of Knossos reveal a man executing a perilous jump on a bull accompanied by the sound of a lyre and a double flute. In the training of wild animals, the Greeks frequently made use of the flute, the drum, and the cithara as a way of calming them.

In Greece an Olympic Stadium was constructed around 780 BC where chariot races were held. This Greek Stadium became in Rome the Circus Maximus, constructed around 600 B.C., ovalshaped, and capable of holding some 150,000 spectators. There, too, the main entertainment was chariot racing. But the Roman structure also possessed a ring, which was not in the center, but located at the extremities of the oval where vaulting on horseback, horses at liberty, juggling, and equilibrists were featured. Rome also had circuses with an enormous ring, such as the Coliseum, where gladiators fought, where wild animals were hunted, and condemned prisoners were offered as prey to wild animals.

Violence was de rigueur. Less violent activities were also presented, such as equestrian acrobatics, juggling, and trained animals. However, while there are some similarities between the Roman circus and the modern circus as established by Philip Astley, according to Antony Hippisley Coxe, it is an error to try to trace the history of the modern circus back to ancient Rome, for the structure of the Roman circus was primarily established with racetracks in mind.

Thus we see that the oval track which lent itself to chariot racing and horse racing, became the nineteenth century Hippodrome, used primarily for the racing of horses at liberty or mounted, (even some *ecuyères* tried their hand at horse racing); the round ring, indispensable to vaulting, acrobatics, or "tricks" on horseback, became the eighteenth century thirteen meter circus ring, which kept the activities of horse and rider within spatial bounds. The various Hippodromes of Paris in the nineteenth century tried to reconcile the oval and the ring by installing a ring in the center of the oval, four lanes emanating from the four sides of the oval, and leading to this center ring.

The physical or spatial aspect of the circus as it was known in Greece or Rome disappeared during the middle Ages. Loosely speaking, one can perhaps say that circus activities as known in the ancient world, were replaced by chivalric tournaments or tourneys during the Middle Ages, (ex: tilting at the ring, tilting at the Quintaine, Carrousels) performed primarily by knights exhibiting their prowess, usually at the various European courts for the entertainment of the king and his court.

However, circus activities as an art form continued to exist and were composed of artists travelling along the roads of Europe, stopping at fairs, at the gates of cities, and at castle gates, eventually leading into the castle court or hall to entertain the lord and lady. These ambulatory artists, wandering from town to town, castle to castle, poor, often hungry and without shelter, were the acrobats, rope dancers, equilibrists, the funambulists, animal trainers, the mimes, puppeteers, and the buffos. Later, the actors who performed tragi-comedies or burlesque plays, often based on Greek and Roman comedies, became the foundation of the Commedia dell' Arte. Théophile Gautier's novel, *Capitaine Fracasse* gives a realistic, yet romanticized, portrayal of the lives of ambulatory actors. All the characters of the Commedia dell' Arte are present in this work. Increasingly popular was the presentation of marionettes, performing dramas, farces, sometimes presenting great spectacles, the latter eventually becoming the main fare in the nineteenth century. A new group joined these puppeteers, namely the illusionists. The Church persecuted the puppeteers and the illusionists, for they often worked on the busy cathedral squares. In fact, all wandering performers were persecuted by the Church. According to Dominique Jando, acrobats were often regarded as possessing magical or supernatural powers. Many an Illusionist was burned to death in public for so-called heresy, for some of them were accused of being members of secret societies such as the Freemasons and the Rosicrucians.

It is interesting to note that the saltimbanques (also known as banquistes or mountebanks) were the original ambulant performers and that from them emanated many famous circus dynasties and famous *écuyers*. To protect themselves these saltimbanques formed an international corporation to aid a needy fellow banquiste. The ambulatory artist was usually an international individual, knowing no frontiers and no racial or ethnic differences. They were wanderers but many were also Wandering Jews, for whom these artistic activities were one of the avenues open to them, making it possible for them to earn their livelihood in relative freedom.

Yet, despite the constant wars, famines, epidemics, and persecution by the Church, as well as by the hostile peasant, "who clings to his chickens" and the rising petit bourgeois, "who clings to his respectability"[1] these wandering artists managed to survive. They survived and remained artists because, despite a rough life, they loved this life which they considered free from the restrictions imposed by society, bowing to no petty ruler or despot. Pierre-Jean de Béranger, a French poet and chansonnier, who lived during the first half of the nineteenth century, understood the life and plight of the wandering artist. In one of his poems he says that these wanderers are: "*Sans pays, sans prince, sans lois, notre vie doit faire envie*" ("Without country, without prince and without laws, our life must be the envy of all.")

Thétard believes that there is a distinction between the wandering artists and another ambulant group travelling along the roads of Europe, namely, the romanies or gypsies. There is, however, disagreement among historians with respect to this distinction. While the romanies did exhibit trained animals (bears, monkeys), they, nonetheless, kept to themselves and were generally not part of the ambulant artist. They, too, went from fair to fair, but primarily to sell the wares they made (utensils, baskets, and other household goods). What they had in common with the travelling artists, the banquistes, was that the romanies, too, were persecuted. They too, cherished their freedom.

These banquistes or travelling artists were born in this cherished environment as described by Béranger, and remained in it for several

---

1   Henry Thétard, *La Merveilleuse Histoire du Cirque*, Paris: Prisma, 1947, Vol I, 19.

generations, knowing little else, or perhaps realizing that there was little else to which they could turn. As Thétard points out, generation followed generation and the various acts remained the same; neither did the names given to these acts ever change.

A type of nobility also developed within these ambulant artists composed of families eventually going back several generations. They knew each other and were often able to recognize each other by their physical appearance. Their backgrounds and places of origin are interesting. According to Thétard, many of these eternal wanderers had their roots in Italian lands, such as Brescia, Parma, or Piacenza. Some even owned ancestral land. Italian names abound within this nobility. And, adds Thétard, it is these people, these ambulant artists who, together with the English and Spanish horsemen, formed the backbone of what became the modern circus in the eighteenth century.[2]

One of the greatest Italian names in the sixteenth century is that of the Chiarini family, whose members appeared already in 1580 at the fairs of Saint-Laurent and Saint-Germain as rope dancers, puppeteers, choreographic mimes and equine acrobats. It is the puppeteer and the mime who took an important place in entertaining both children and adults. While le Baron de Vaux in his work *Écuyers et Ecuyères* says that it was in the 1830s that we see the rise of the *ecuyère*, Angelica Chiarini was already working as an *ecuyère* of note in 1784 in Astley's Royal Amphitheatre, then in Paris with Antonio Franconi. Another woman, Constance Chiarini, also became famous for performing *haute école* (she married the Russian Count Rospotchine).

Other great dynasties soon developed such as the Franconi dynasty, the Lalanne dynasty, the Renz dynasty, the Knie dynasty, the Schumann dynasty. Many members of these dynasties had originally been saltimbanques who became famous *écuyer*s or circus directors. In England famous names such as Bradbury or Clarke Cook, also established famous families of saltimbanques and are mentioned in the annals of the famous variety theater, Sadler's Wells, first opened in 1683. Many of these saltimbanques appeared in Philip Astley's circus.[3]

While companies of acrobats, rope dancers, equestrian acrobats, equilibrists, puppeteers, funambulists were crossing and recrossing Europe, increasing their numbers, expanding their acts, performing at fairs, outside the gates of cities and castles, or, if they had the means, in little theaters of sailcloth or wood, a new kind of theater developed in England in 1770. This new type of theater eventually became the

---

2 *Ibid.*, 31.

3 *Ibid.*, 32.

circus as we know it today. It is only with this newly founded type of entertainment in 1770 that the term "circus" and all that it entails can be used legitimately.

A young man, Philip Astley, son of a cabinetmaker, had initially joined His Majesty's cavalry. In 1766, at the age of twenty-four, he resigned from the army as sergeant-major. Taking advantage of his riding skills, in 1768 he rented a field named Halfpenny Hatch near Westminster Bridge and performed before Londoners, vaulting on two or three horses, while simultaneously performing saber maneuvers. These acts were reminiscent of cavalry exercises. In 1770 Astley moved his activities to a corner of Bridge Road and Stangate Street, just opposite Westminster Bridge. The performances did not vary. Astley, dressed as a dragoon, on his horse, Gibraltar, performed military charges, as well as the saber attacks and defenses of the Hussars. But he also performed nonmilitary acts such as vaulting on two or three horses. Two *ecuyères*, his wife and a Miss Vangable, as well as his son, all three competent riders, were added to the programme

To these equestrian performances, Astley very soon included acrobats, jugglers, and, of course, clowns. One of Astley's early comic episodes gave the clown a military and equestrian aspect. Here the equestrian clowning took the form of a regimental tailor who was ill-fitted to ride on the back of a horse. One can well imagine the trials and tribulations the poor tailor had to experience in his attempt to get on the back of a horse and ride. This burlesque episode appeared later in Paris with the Cirque Franconi. After this initial and short-lived equestrian clowning, the clown performed on foot, which was his usual mode of locomotion. According to Dominique Jando, it was the clown in Shakespeare's theater who served Astley as model.

Soon Astley, still out in the open, traced a thirteen meter circular ring, erected wooden seats for the spectators, and, to the equestrian acts, added companies of rope dancers, acrobats, and tumblers. Thus the first modern circus was born. In 1779 an amphitheater was built of wood and called Astley's Royal Amphitheatre of Arts. When the building burned down, a new building was erected with a ring for equestrian acts, acrobatics, and other acts, encircled by stepped rows of seats; a stage was added at one end where there were no seats and which was to serve as a theater for pantomimes and other non-equestrian acts.

But Astley, while very successful in England, looked for greener pastures: France, where he had on a few occasions given the same kind of performances he had given in London. In 1782 he acquired land in the Faubourg du Temple where he erected the first Parisian circus. During the Napoleonic Wars he re-enlisted and fought under the command of the Duke of York. After the war he returned to Paris in 1814. He died that same year and was buried in the Père Lachaise cemetery. In 1802 Astley's *A System of Equestrian Education* appeared. Astley was not only interested in performing equestrian acts in the evenings, he also taught equitation in the mornings.

D.L. Murray in his introduction to M. Willson Disher's *Greatest Show on Earth* firmly believes that "Astley is [the circus'] real founder whatever Roman gladiators or medieval jousters may have done..."[4]

Eventually the Astley Amphitheatre was taken over by Antonio Franconi, founder and chief of the Franconi dynasty.

Antonio Franconi was born in 1737 in Undine (or in Venice in 1739?) to Blasio and Julia Franconi. As legend has it, at the age of twenty-three Antonio killed a patrician of Venice in a duel and escaped to France. He arrived in Lyon penniless. In order to survive he became a handler of animals with a travelling menagerie, where he tried to tame and train a young lion who bit him in the arm. Undaunted, Antonio would have continued in this work and even been successful, had he not fought and injured another employee who was envious of his skill and success. He took off once again with a small amount of money in his pocket with which he bought a few birds which he proceeded to train. He then went to Spain where bull-fighting had become a popular spectator sport. He became enthused and returned to France with the idea of fighting bulls in France. He married and had two sons, Laurent and Henri. Fortunately bull-fighting came to naught and in 1783 he performed with his birds at Astley's Amphitheatre which had opened in 1782 in the Faubourg du Temple. Antonio soon became Astley's associate.

During the French Revolution of 1789 and the Revolutionary Wars conducted by those countries which continued to possess crowned heads, together with the exiles, mostly aristocrats who had fled France to form the Armée des Princes (also known as l'Armée de Condé), Astley's Amphitheatre was left unattended. In 1793 it became Antonio's Amphitheatre. Soon it became known as the first Cirque Olympique.

During the Third Phase of the Revolution, begun approximately in 1793, the most intolerant and bloody period, Antonio got into trouble with the Revolutionary authorities for hiding the very nobleman who had helped him financially when he was penniless. Antonio became a suspect and when he happened to be out of town, the poor nobleman

---

4   Willson Disher, *The Greatest Show on Earth*, London: G.Bell & Sons, 1937, X.

was caught and taken to prison. Shortly thereafter, Antonio had a shoot out with the authorities who, this time, came to apprehend him. They left; threatening to return but never did so. Antonio left town for a while and returned after Robespierre's downfall.

When the Revolution was over and France was ruled by the Five Sires who sat rather precariously in the governmental saddle, the doors of the Amphitheatre Franconi opened on 25 November 1795. In 1807 it became the first Cirque Olympique.

Of the Franconi dynasty, Thétard says that "the Franconi, Venetian *gentilshommes* (men of gentle birth) became French *gentilshommes*."[5] More importantly, says Thétard, the history of the Franconi dynasty is also the history of the circus.

Indeed, the Franconi dynasty is an astonishing phenomenon. It not only furthered Astley's circus and, eventually, formed its own circuses, its members performing *haute école* and vaulting, but was also instrumental in training horses, teaching the art of equitation to the many *ecuyères* who performed in the Franconi circus and other circuses of Paris and the capitals of Europe.

Antonio with his two sons, Laurent and Henri, appeared on the programme of their circus. Much of the programme consisted of acrobatic equitation. But *haute école* was also introduced, an act which had never appeared during the Astley period in London. Antonio had learned the principles and movements of *haute école* in Italy, an art that had originated in Spain, and which was practiced by all the gentilshommes of Italy in the eighteenth century. He had imparted these principles to his sons Laurent and Henri.

While at first Laurent had performed vaulting and did all kinds of acrobatics on horseback, he became an even better horseman than his father in the art of *haute école*. When in 1815, during the restoration of the Ancìen regime which placed the old monarchy back in the saddle, he took lessons from Abzac the director of the briefly re-opened École de Versailles, which closed its doors permanently in 1830.

Laurent Franconi was, as has been noted, well-versed in Classical or academic equitation. But when he practiced it himself in the circus and imparted its principles to his sons, he rid it of much of its superfluous aspects, that is, those aspects that had been taught in the sixteenth and seventeenth centuries by Antoine de Pluvinel and Salomon de La Brou, as well as by the many *écuyers* throughout the existence of the École de Versailles which had been established by Louis XIV in 1680. Now stirrup leathers were shortened so that legs no longer

---

5   Thétard, *ibid.*, 66.

First Astley Amphiteatre, 1808.

dangled down with toes pointed downwards, as they did at the École de Versailles, and the saddle became more streamlined. Thus shorter stirrup leathers and a less cumbersome saddle gave the rider a more solid seat.

Many of these changes introduced by Franconi, were also being introduced by former *écuyer*s of the École de Versailles, who now taught equitation to the "jeunesse dorée" (gilded youth) in the established commercial *manège*s, for these new Parisian riders wanted mostly to ride in the Bois de Boulogne or at Rambouillet.

It should be mentioned that *manège* riding had already been transformed by former *écuyer*s who, though trained at the École de Versailles, had, already in the eighteenth century, opted for a freer and less cumbersome style of riding, namely military riding, a much freer kind of riding both for horse as well as for rider, better suited for the cavalry or military.

Laurent was an imposing figure on horseback executing *haute école*, dressed severely in his grey *haut-de-forme* and his blue redingote. When General L'Hotte saw him in Saumur in 1845, he said "there is majesty on horseback."

One of the attractions of the Cirque Olympique was the re-introduction of the tailor episode, a burlesque and simple pantomime. The tailor was now a Gascon who, like his former English "victim," was incapable of sitting on a horse. In the Franconi version, the tailor was persecuted by the horse right into his shop.

Both Laurent and Henri and their wives, and Laurent Lalanne, who belonged to an ancient dynasty, executed equestrian exercises. One of Laurent's acts of 1808 was the "Strength of Hercules." Two horses were brought into the arena. Laurent took hold of their bridles, placing one foot in a stirrup of each horse. Two *ecuyères*, the wives of Laurent and Henri, stood on their respective horses, while three *écuyers* formed a pyramid on the shoulders of Laurent who, departing at the canter, supported all of them. In a similar act called the "Croix à Quatre," Laurent carried his brother, Henri, on his shoulders and, by means of a belt, and he held his wife and his sister-in-law.

In addition to equestrian acts, the Franconi circus presented pantomimes, clowns, acrobats, rope-dancers. The Franconi brothers sometimes performed in comic pieces, as well as exhibited trained animals, such as Kioumi and Baba the elephants and Coco a stag. Coco could leap over eight men and four horses. He had also been taught to stand still while a pistol was fired between his antlers.

The pantomimes were usually of a comic nature, fitting the equestrian mode better than could either drama or tragedy. Many of these acts had initially been performed by Andrew Ducrow who had become director of Astley's Amphitheater: "The Adventures of Don Quichotte," "Two Englishmen in a *manège*," "The Lantern of Diogenes." Eventually military pantomimes and military glories, dealing with the exploits of the French armies, the "Taking of the Bastille," the "Empire of the One Hundred Days," and glorious feats of Napoleon were performed. These spectacles became very popular with the public.

At times animals played the main roles while humans were relegated to secondary roles. For example, in "Don Quichote," Don Quichote and Sancho Panza were eclipsed by the horse, Rosinante, and the donkey. In the "Bataille d'Aboukir," "the horses acted a very moving drama of devoted courage,"[6] saving the lives of their masters.

The two young Franconis, Laurent and Henri, became the rage of Paris and many members of Le Tout-Paris took equitation lessons from them. It was with the Franconis that, according to Thétard, the heroic era of the French circus began.

The Franconi circus moved several times. When an area in which the circus had been established became too busy, as for example, the development of the fashionable Rue de la Paix, they moved to the Rue Saint-Honoré. Eventually the second Cirque Olympique was established in 1817, then the third in 1827. In addition to a ring, there was also a stage for pantomimes or hippodramas.

---

6   Disher, *ibid.*, 170.

But it was with the second Cirque Olympique, when the circus became fashionable with all the social classes, that the horse, together with the *écuyer* or écuyére, really became king.

At the age of ninety, Antonio could be seen sitting in his special seat, watching his sons and grandsons ride. When he died, 6 December 1836, his last horse was decked in black and silver, followed by family, friends, and Le Tout-Paris.

Unfortunately, the Franconi brothers were not always very successful as businessmen, for their main concern was the furthering of art, especially equestrian art, and the funds they had amassed were often depleted, despite the fact that many prominent persons had subscribed to its support, including King Charles X. While they took in a considerable amount of money every night, they were often unable to break even, due, in part, to the fact that they were involved in a number of unsuccessful experiments. The Directorship was then given to Louis Dejean who owned the land on which the circus stood. The opening of a second circus in 1835, The Cirque des Champs-Elysées, contributed to Dejean's success, but did not contribute to the financial success of the Franconi brothers. Henri retired to his property and Laurent traveled to the capitals of Europe performing *haute école*.

Throughout the many decades after its establishment, the Cirque des Champs-Elysées became Paris' most brilliant circus, especially with respect to equestrian virtuosity. Many of the *ecuyères* who will be discussed later had, at some time or other, demonstrated their equestrian talent at the Cirque des Champs-Elysées. In fact the Cirque des Champs-Elysées must be considered "the conservatory of the ring, the temple of equitation, and an art which, at the time, was in all its brilliance in France."[7]

During the 1840s Paris became the capital of the circus world. Each night the hall of the Cirque des Champs-Elysées was filled with the "lionnes" (the fashionable women) of Paris, now sitting in more comfortable seats. Many a "lion" or dandy stood in the corridors that led to the stables, ready to ogle with their lorgnons [opera glasses] the *ecuyères* as they entered the ring.

The famous clown, Jean-Baptiste Auriol (1806-1881), performed at the Cirque des Champs-Elysées. Auriol, says Thétard, was the complete artist. He was a funambulist, an equilibrist, a jumper, one of the first to perform with the "batoude," a springboard from which a perilous jump, starting from the wings, ended in the ring itself.

It was also in 1839 and the early 1840s when François Baucher

---

7   Thétard,*ibid.*,89.

Arena and stage of the third Astley Amphiteatre, 1817.

riding Partisan and Caroline Loyo riding Rutler on alternate nights, brought the public, especially Le Tout-Paris, to the circus. Very soon the already popular Cuzent family appeared, with Paul Cuzent as head of the company composed of his sisters Antoinette, Armantine, and Pauline, and Antoinette's husband, Jean Lejars.

Laurent Lalanne performed "The Royal Post" as did the brothers Baptiste and François Loisset to rousing applause. In "The Royal Post," the *écuyer* stood on two horses, letting several other horses, one at a time (sometimes as many as twelve), pass through his legs, immediately snatching up the reins of each horse as it passed underneath him and which he then proceeded to drive with long lines. The horses represented the countries through which the couriers had to pass, sometimes bearing banners on their backs with the names of these countries. Paul Cuzent went one step farther and stood on four horses.

Virginie Kenebel, who later married Victor Franconi, was another famous *ecuyère de panneau* performing at the time at the Cirque des Champs-Elysées.

Initiated by the brothers Loisset, together with Pierre Monfroid, complete somersaults were performed on moving horses in single file, known as a salto mortaje, a perilous jump.

The greatness of Laurent Franconi became legendary. There is the famous story recounted by many writers when, in 1843, Laurent Franconi came to Saumur with his company. The Commandant de Novital of the Ecole de Cavalerie had put at Laurent's disposal the small *manège* in which his company could perform. It should be noted that Novital was a bauchériste. Novital knew at what time Laurent rode in the morning and wanted to return a courtesy visit that Laurent had made the previous day. He rode his horse Omphaly to the *manège*. Indeed, Laurent was already riding his horse Norma. After the usual preliminary greetings and compliments, Laurent asked Novital to ride his mare Norma.

"But it is for you to ride Omphaly," said Novital. "I am at home here and I am asking you to do me this honor."

Laurent Franconi, taking advantage of the honor made to him by his host, dismounted Norma and got on Omphaly. Laurent executed wonders with Omphaly, the horse François Baucher had trained for Novital. In fact he rode much better than did Baucher. In turn Laurent Franconi offered Norma to Novital who got on him with a certain amount of emotion, for so great was his admiration for the *écuyer* of *haute école*, Laurent Franconi, whose outstanding movements on Omphaly he had just witnessed. Commandant de Novital, after having studied Norma's advantages and disadvantages for a while, had the mare execute movements so perfectly that Laurent called out:

"You are, indeed, a master."[8]

And so it goes when two great riders recognize each other's equestrian and artistic excellence.

Indeed, the horses trained by Laurent Franconi always achieved such a degree of excellence and finesse so that when Laurent asked them certain movements, his position and seat remained academically perfect and his aids were imperceptible. His touch was so delicate, reminiscent of la Guérinière's "delicate touch with the spur."[9] Laurent knew how to appraise his horse's strength, how to regularize his gaits, how to sustain his equilibrium; he also knew that he should never tire a horse needlessly, especially when performing the high airs.

To vary equestrian performances Laurent and Henri also presented, as noted, burlesque scenes on horseback, such as "The regiment's tailor" or "The Regiment's Dog," and many others. Soon burlesque scenes became more elaborate spectacles. Many were

---

8   Baron de Vaux, *Écuyers et Ecuyères*, Paris: J. Rothschild, 1893, 302. Also quoted by Thétard, Vol I, 34.

9   Vaux, *ibid.*, 302.

military glories or dramas, such as "The Attack on the Convoy," or extravaganzas based on Napoleonic legends, Greek or Roman myths, which were very successful with the public. One pantomime was called "The Lantern of Diogenes" which represented Diogenes looking, with his lantern, for a great man throughout the ages and finally stopping in front of the bust of Napoleon. He had, indeed, found the great man. Also popular was the legend of "Mazeppa or the Wild Horse of Tartary," a somewhat dangerous act as the rider had to be tightly bound to the back of a galloping horse. Jenny de Rhaden had, much against her will, performed this act towards the end of the century. But the rider best known for this dangerous act was Adah Isaacs Menken.

In 1843 Laurent and his son, Victor, founded the first modern Hippodrome near the Place de l'Etoile, representing a totally new genre, far removed from the Classical equestrian circus as delineated by Astley. The building was vast and had a track that was in the form of an elongated ellipse, able to seat 12,000 spectators. Horse racing at liberty, obstacle racing, *amazone* racing became a specialty. Elaborate pantomimes were presented. Eventually, like so many circus buildings, the building burned down.

In 1877 the Hippodrome de l'Alma was built with Charles Zidler serving as its director. Its roof was made of glass and could be opened during warm summer nights. Extravagant pantomimes were also performed dealing with Joan of Arc, a pantomime in three acts, Nero, and other historical and mythological figures.

Henri Franconi wrote a number of pantomimes, such as "Cain ou le premier crime," "Clarisse et Lovelace ou le séducteur", "La Dame du Lac ou l'Inconnue." Théophile Gautier's novel, mentioned earlier, became an *opéra-comique* written by Catulle Mendès, performed at the Cirque 01ympique in July 1878.

The great Laurent died in 1849 of the cholera shortly after the establishment of the Hippodrome de l'Etoile. A few months later his brother, Henri, died of the same disease. Several cholera epidemics and pandemics had gripped Europe during the mid-century, taking the lives of many.

After the sudden death of the two brothers, Laurent and Henri, the two circuses, the Cirque Olympique and the Cirque des Champs-Elysées, which became known as Les Deux Cirques, went back to the directorship of Laurent's son Victor.

Victor Franconi was, like his father Laurent, also a remarkable horseman, capable of riding untried green horses as well as trained ones. Vaux tells us that he saw "Victor get on horses whom he did not know and after having worked with them for a brief moment, managed to get remarkable work out of them. It often happened that he sometimes bought difficult horses, almost all were difficult, and he put them through the *manège* airs in a relatively short time."[10] According to Vaux "Victor Franconi, together with Aure, Baucher, and Pellier, was one of those men who achieved the most for outdoor and *manège* equitation."[11] It was at Les Deux Cirques that *haute école*, academic or savant horsemanship, was practiced and studied. Victor Franconi is also the author of *Le Cavalier et l'écuyer.*

He died in 1897 at the age of eighty-seven. Madame Victor Franconi, the former sylphe Virginie Kenebel, the *ecuyère de panneau* to whom many a poet had dedicated his verses, told Thétard that throughout Victor's illness he had been saddened by the decline of the circus.

In fact, by 1880, the public had begun to be bored with equestrian performances. To retain the fickle public, Victor Franconi had introduced such acts as aerial gymnastics and had added more acrobatics. Equestrian acts became less prominent.

The Cirque d'Hiver had become the great competitor. Established in 1852 by Dejean to replace the Cirque Olympique destroyed by Haussman's city planning, it went through name changes as the country went through political changes. It was first called the Cirque Napoleon when Louis Napoleon became Emperor Napoleon III; after the downfall of Napoleon in 1870 it became the Cirque National, then, in 1873 the Cirque d'Hiver with Victor Franconi as its director. However, equestrian traditions were still strong with Emilie and Clotilde Loisset, and James Fillis gracing the circus with their equestrian excellence. It was in 1882 when, on that fatal day, Emilie Loisset was crushed to death by her horse. Many saw this as a bad omen for the equestrian circus.

Eventually the Cirque d'Eté was torn down and the Cirque d'Hiver was losing money, for the circus had difficulty holding its own in its battle with a certain loss of interest on the part of the public, as well as competition with those newer institutions of entertainment such as the Folies-Bergère and the many musichalls, which also presented circus acts.

When Victor Franconi died at the age of 86 in his home at 32, Boulevard du Temple and his body taken to the Père Lachaise cemetery, one can say that his death influenced the Cirque d'Hiver. Presentations of acrobats, jugglers, trapeze artists, equilibristes, pantomimes, became more pronounced. Replacing *haute école* were equestrian acrobats,

---

10 Ibid., 303.

11 Ibid., 303.

usually riding bareback and performing somersaults, and acts with horses at liberty.

In 1898, Victor's son, Charles, abandoned the Cirque des Champs-Elysées and the building was torn down. Flowerbeds replaced the building. However, at the very spot where the circus' ring had been located, that spot remained (and still remains) bare and children could play (and still do) where Baucher, Loyo, Cuzent and others had once triumphed.

At the end of the century three circuses remained in Paris: the Cirque d'Hiver directed by Charles Franconi, the Cirque Fernando, which became the Cirque Medrano in 1893, the Nouveau Cirque in the rue Saint-Honoré, not too far from the first Franconi circus, the Cirque Olympique. Nonetheless, as R. Toole-Stott says, these circuses "reflected only a shadow of their former glory."[12] The Brothers Bouglione took over the Cirque d'Hiver in the 1930s, which is still very much alive today. Posters prominently announcing a number of acts were displayed in front of the building in October 2000. Above all, the equestrian statue of La Belle Madame Lejars and her horse Thisby continues to command the facade in the Faubourg du Temple. I saluted her.

Four generations of the Franconi dynasty witnessed the rise and decline of the equestrian circus, that is, the circus as it had first been established at Westminster Bridge in 1770 and at the Faubourg du Temple in 1782. It rose with the first Franconi, Antoine, and declined with the last of the Franconis.

And just as romanticism, artistic and literary, faded as the century ran its course to become so-called realism, naturalism, symbolism (and other isms, all complex and difficult to define), so did many aspects of the circus, especially the part played by its romantic *ecuyères*, gradually disappear, to be replaced by perhaps more appropriate human beings and human endeavors for the new era. Hughes Le Roux, Tristan Rémy, and Adrian were well aware of a certain romanticism that had surrounded the circus, especially the lives of many of these nineteenth century *ecuyères*. This concept has been beautifully expressed by Le Roux when he refers to that "troubling beauty of a woman on a horse, this plastic coupling of two curvilinears that are the most perfect creation: the stallion, aggrandizing woman in all her majesty; woman on the creature she rides, posed audaciously like a wing."[13]

---

12   R. Toole-Stott, *Circus and Allied Arts—A World Bibliography*, Darbey, England: Harpur & Sons, 1958, Vol.1, 15.

13   Hughes Le Roux, *Les Jeux du Cirque et la vie foraine,* Paris: E. Plon,

> *L'Histoire du cheval est celle de l'humanìté.*
> The history of the horse is the history of mankind.
> (Dr. C. Chomeì, nineteenth century veterinarian)

> *Cut the dialect (dialogue) and come to the 'osses.*
> (Andrew Ducrow, equestrian acrobat, Director of Astley's Amphitheater, uttered these words at a rehearsal of Hamlet.)

CHAPTER II:
THE HORSE IS KING IN THE CIRCUS

The title of Adrian Jacob Severe Russ' (usually known as Adrian) book, *Le Cirque commence... à cheval* (The Circus begins on... horseback) underlines the importance of the horse in the circus. "The horse," says Adrian, "is the 'old man' of the spectacle and when one realizes that the entire structure of the modern circus was conceived with him in mind, there is no doubt that he is the first father of the ring."[14] This does not imply that the horse was not used in earlier times, for example, in Classical antiquity, and that there were not horsemen executing acrobatic feats. But the special use of the horse in the circus, with dimensions specifically made to accommodate him and his rider, was really an eighteenth century reality. The very dimensions of the ring, namely thirteen meters in diameter, as initially traced by Philip Astley, were set primarily to accommodate vaulting and other acrobatic acts on the horse. Indeed, the horse was king.

Henry Thétard also considers the horse the backbone of the circus, (as does Josef von Halperson), but juxtaposes to the horse the human element and that together they formed "the backbone of the circus."[15]

Initially only *haute école* equitation was to have been presented and discussed in this work. However, I included Antoinette Jolibois-Cuzent-Lejars because she was a very popular, daring, and outstanding *ecuyère de panneau* and the sister of Pauline Cuzent, usually working and travelling with her. Furthermore, many of the *ecuyères* performing

---

Nourrit et Cie,1889, 120-121.

14   Adrian, *Le Cirque commence à cheval,* Bourg-Ia-Reine: Adrian, 1968, 43.

15   Henry Thétard, *La Merveilleuse Histoire du cirque*, Paris:Prisma, 1947, Vol. i, 165

haute école in the circus also included in their programmes movements that were more typical of the circus, that is, they included acrobatic skills or "tricks" on their horses.

I also included Marie-Isabelle, an *ecuyère* who did not perform in the circus. I did so because she briefly "taught" officers and non-commissioned officers and "trained" horses at the Ecole de Cavalerie of Saumur, and because Vaux referred to her as an *ecuyère* and included her in his book on *écuyers* and *ecuyères*.

There were three or perhaps even four kinds of equestrian activities occurring in the circuses of the nineteenth century:

1. Vaulting and equestrian acrobatics.

Here the human being, through acrobatic skills, was the main attraction. The horse was merely the secondary actor, the tool. These acts were often dangerous, sometimes fatal. The horse used for vaulting or acrobatic skills was, understandably, of a heavier conformation than the horse used for *haute école* or at liberty. Also important were the dimensions of the horse's top line, from back to croup, to make acrobatics easier and safer.

The horse used by the *écuyer* who performed acrobatic stunts or the *ecuyère de panneau* who performed either as a ballerina or as an acrobat, usually was a sure-footed creature with gaits that were well-connected. He had to have a steady canter with short even paces, and be able to keep a strict tempo. The horse's regularity of movement was very important, for the slightest mis-movement of the horse could upset the rider's equilibrium.

There were varied types of vaulting or equestrian acrobatics. The difficult and dangerous acts were usually performed by men, as, for example, the salto mortale, which involved double jumps from horse to horse sometimes moving in single file; the movement known as "voltige à la Richard"; the formation of a pyramid on horseback, the "Strength of Hercules," "The Royal Post" or "The Courier of Saint-Petersburg," and many others. The *ecuyère* usually became a dancer on her horse, or she jumped through hoops, or danced with scarves, or veils, or, from her horse, picked up a scarf or a flower that lay on the ground. As Adrian says, when it comes to the *ecuyère*, strength became grace. She danced on a panneau which made her work easier. She usually wore a tutu, later, tights. Often a pas de deux was danced when an *écuyer* arrived on the scene and joined the equestrian ballerina.

However, many *ecuyères* also performed more demanding acrobatic feats on their mounts, as was the case of Antoinette Jolibois-

Cuzent-Lejars and her sister Armantine. Even *ecuyères* of *haute école* such as Elise Petzold, Fanny Ghyga, Jenny de Rhaden, and, especially, Blanche Allarty, performed often dangerous acrobatic feats on their horses.

The first vaulting performance was described by Louis Emile Campardon in 1775 in his erudite book entitled *Les Spectacles* de *la Foire* which deals with artists of all kinds: jumpers, rope dancers, dwarfs, giants, marionettes, mechanical toys, performing at the Fairs of Saint-Germain and Saint-Laurent. The first vaulting performance described by Campardon is mentioned by Thétard. This description deals with two partners, an Englishman named Hyam and a French *ecuyère* named Masson. Both used saddles when vaulting. Masson first entered the ring at a gallop, standing with one foot on the saddle, the other foot between the horse's ears; or sometimes she stood on two horses, jumping over a fence. Hyam performed the same vaulting movements but he executed somersaults on the horse's back, or over the horse's body. He also jumped over obstacles on two horses, carrying a child on his back, passing from one horse to the other.[16]

Hughes Le Roux believes that of the many kinds of uses to which the human and the equine were put in the circus, the most dangerous was vaulting or equestrian acrobatics. "Ask the true artistes *de panneau*, a Jenny O'Brien, for instance, what they think of this kind of acrobatics...and they will not hesitate to admit that if jumping is a sure way of getting applause, it is the worst way of satisfying the conscience of an artist." Indeed, adds Le Roux, "danger adds a certain amount of greatness to effort, for it is to the *ecuyère* a panneau that the public is drawn most instinctively and extends its greatest enthusiasm."[17]

An extension of equine acrobatics were pantomimes or hippodramas. At first they were relatively simple, becoming more and more extravagant, eventually reaching mythic and legendary proportions. According to A.H. Saxon, "In the history of hippodramas or hippodramatic entertainment, one play towers above all others, Mazeppa..."[18]

Initially Mazeppa or the Wild Horse of Tartary was an incident in Voltaire's, *Histoire* de *Charles XII.*

---

16 *Ibid.*, 165.

17 Hughes Le Roux, *Les Jeux du cirque et la vie foraine*, Paris: E. Plon, Nourrit et Cie, 134.

18 A. H. Saxon, *Enter Foot and Horse, A History of Hippodramas in England and France*, New Haven: Yale University Press, 1978, 173.

It then became a poem by Lord Byron. As it changed genres, it also changed, to some extent, plot, characters, ambiance, but always retaining the tartarean aspect of hero and horse.

In the initial story Mazeppa, punished for his indiscretions with the Fung of Poland's wife, was bound to the back of a wild horse of Tartary who galloped off for his homeland through fields, forests, across rivers, pursued by wolves and by curious wild horses. Finally the horse fell down and died from exhaustion on the steppes of Tartary with Mazeppa still tied to his back. Throughout much of the wild journey, Mazeppa was unconscious, having fainted from pain and exposure.

Byron's poem eventually went through several different genres and versions, first performed as plays or hippodramas with little equestrian activity. It had a brief period of success in England in 1823, then found its way to France where it appealed to J.G.A. Cuvelier de Trie who, with Leopold Chandezon, rewrote the work. It received its premiere at the Cirque Olympique 11 January 1825. In this version Mazeppa, known as Casimir, was in love with Olinska, the daughter of the Polish Castellan, and was allowed to demonstrate his equestrian excellence when he displayed his mastery over a wild Tartarean horse and received the trophy of victory from the hands of his beloved.

He, too, eventually had to gallop through steppes, forests, lakes, and other wild scenery. To express this furious gallop, the horse actually had to gallop furiously across the stage with Mazeppa tied to his back. After many trials and tribulations Mazeppa was rescued and

Double somersault—*salto mortale*.

Ecuyère de panneau

proclaimed King of Tartary and "mounted on a white courser which none but a Khan can ride, prepares to lead the Tartars against the hated Poles and rescue his beloved Olinska."[19] In this French version at the Cirque Olympique, Mazeppa was able to display his equestrian excellence slightly more than in the earlier ones.

After having achieved reasonable success in France, the hippodrama returned to England where it was rewritten in two more versions. In the Milner version Mazeppa was clothed in short white trunks and leggings, his upper body covered in brown cloth rather than wearing the earlier military dress. When Mazeppa appeared on the scene, the wild Tartarean horse had already been brought to center stage "rearing and kicking and dragging three or four grooms who, with the greatest difficulty, tried to restrain it..."[20] The scenery was composed of precipitous mountain ridges, abounding with cataracts, reminiscent of the scenery of a gothic novel. The path the horse and rider had to traverse was very treacherous "zigzagging from the stage floor to the very flies."[21] Rather than endanger both horse and rider, a second horse with a dummy on his back actually made the ascent. During the many productions of Mazeppa, a number of accidents occurred for both horse and rider.

Mazeppa was also very popular in the United States. As in England and France, in the United States the role of Mazeppa was

---

19   *Ibid.*, 177.

20   *Ibid.*, 182.

21   *Ibid.*, 182.

Horse and rider on tightrope.

played by a man. Soon, however, it occurred to one of the managers that perhaps a woman playing the role of Mazeppa would have more box office appeal. The actress chosen for the role was Adah Isaaks Menken. "Her round boyish face and provocatively contoured body were certain to draw the town..."[22] She first performed the role in New York in 1862. The use of a dummy was dispensed with and Adah and the horse had to perform the dangerous trek from stage to flies. On one occasion horse and rider fell off the runway. Fortunately both soon recovered. Adah became a sensation for the danger thrilled the spectator as did the costume she wore.

Adah then sailed from San Francisco to England in April 1864. She played the role of Mazeppa at Astley's Royal Amphitheatre for ten weeks. She then went to Paris. It was in December 1866 that Paris was able to see the long awaited "Naked Lady" at the Gaité (a photograph shows that she is far from being naked). She met Alexandre Dumas, père, and a brief romantic liaison occurred. After a brief success in Mazeppa and other plays and hippodramas in Paris, she returned to London in 1867 where she continued to perform, meeting some of England's poets. Adah, herself, wrote poetry.

But Adah's health began to fail. Soon her illness affected her performance. She returned to Paris to act in Les Pirates de Savanne,

---

22 *Ibid.*, 191.

Mazeppa or The Wild Horse of Tartary—a hippodrama.

but after the second rehearsal she was unable to go on. She died in August 1868 at the age of thirty-three. She was buried in Père Lachaise cemetery. The following year the Rothschild family had her body removed to Montparnasse.

Other women have attempted the role of Mazeppa, especially in England and in the United States. In France it was no longer a full-length hippodrama; only the "chevauchée de Mazeppa," that is, the long trek from stage to flies, was featured. The majority of these productions took place at the Theatre du Châtelet. In 1878 the "chevauchée" was revived with the tightrope artist Océana Renz. In 1883 "Anna Ken... made hearts palpitate as she prepared for the daring ride to the flies."[23] When the horse refused to go any faster than a walk, a pack of mastiffs were unleashed to chase him up the ramps. Jenny de Rhaden was also talked into playing the role of Mazeppa. After she performed *haute école* in her distinguished looking *amazone* attire, she "dutifully disrobed and revealed her charms for the sensational ride up the ramps."[24] In her autobiography, Jenny refers to this production, saying that she went through the performance with great reluctance and concern.

It became quite obvious that by now the drama itself counted for little. It was the daring "chevauchée de Mazeppa" that was

23   *Ibid.*, 203.
24   *Ibid.*, 203.

presented by the various directors and managers.

Another interesting hippodrama, written by Cuvelier de Trie as vaudeville in one act was "Le Boulevard du Temple." It was written to inaugurate the new hall of the Cirque Olympique in 1817 and intended to be a curtain raiser. What was interesting about this vaudeville was the dialogue discussing the nature and appeal of the circus.

2. Horses at liberty

This is perhaps the most demanding kind of act on the part of both horse and trainer, although not necessarily the most dangerous. This type of equine performance requires considerable rapport between horse and trainer, requiring patience, skill, and psychology, and a basket or a large pocket filled with carrots. During a performance when the horse is at liberty, he is, in a sense, on his own, executing movements by means of the trainer's lunging whip and, most importantly, his or her voice. There is no rider who can make use of imperceptible aids to guide the horse. It is not always easy to determine in which of the categories one should place the *savant* (learned) horse. Here, too, this horse is not mounted; one could say he is at liberty. He is usually a comedian. He plays at being wounded, eating in a restaurant, opening a champagne bottle, and going to bed or is already settled in bed. Or the horse depicts such facial traits as amusement, joy, indifference, or anger.[25]

In the nineteenth century Leopold Loyal was one of the best-known trainers of horses at liberty and the savant horse. The trainer placed himself in the center of the ring, an aid stood on the sidelines, a riding whip in hand. If the horse complied with the demands of the trainer, he was given a carrot, if he resisted, the aid jumped forward and smacked him on the appropriate area. Thus, as Vaux points out, the secret of training horses at liberty was the whip and the carrot. It is interesting to note that it was the trainer who administered the carrot, the aid, the whip. It is not too difficult to make a horse rear, since rearing is what a horse often does. All the trainer has to do is place himself in front of the horse, agitate the riding whip close to his nose and, with his right hand, crack the lunge whip. However, while the horse rears without much difficulty, he dislikes kneeling or lying down at the whim of his trainer. To accomplish this feat, bracelets were placed above the hoof, to which a rope was attached. At a given moment, the trainer, when he got the attention of the horse by means

---

25 Adrian, ibid., 40.

of his voice, quickly pulled at the rope, making the horse raise his leg, thereby destroying his equilibrium.

He then quickly threw the horse on to the ground by means of a vigorous push at the shoulder. Eventually the horse no longer needed bracelet or rope; nor did he have to be pushed to the ground. He lay down of his own accord when he noticed the trainer near him and heard him shout. A similar procedure was used to make a horse kneel. According to Monsieur Loyal, it was most difficult to make a horse at liberty execute lead changes. It took about a year for the horse to accomplish this movement. But thanks to his outstanding memory, a horse eventually can learn to do all these tricks.

While it is clear how a horse, with a trainer's skill, patience, whip, and carrots, can be made to lie down, kneel, and execute lead changes, it is difficult to understand how a horse can be made to express different moods such as anger, amusement, or indifference. There is, however, a photograph in Renevey's *Le Grand Livre du Cirque* which shows a horse laughing cynically, with two clowns near his shoulder, also laughing.

3. *Haute école*

It was primarily Laurent Franconi who stressed *haute école* in the circus. In pure *haute école*, that is, Classical, academic, equitation savante, the horse is equal to the rider, or should perhaps, even be the most important partner, giving the impression that he is acting on his own, that is, he is on parole. The emphasis should be on the horse. The rider of *haute école* should efface himself or herself, should appear passive, and the use of aids should be imperceptible, even unnecessary. In the circus, while the horse is equal to the rider, the rider often acts in a more dramatic, even frenzied manner, at times giving the impression that the particular movement is difficult to achieve, sometimes even making the horse attempt the movement a few times before succeeding. In pure *haute école*, the rider should impart the impression that the movements the rider and the horse are executing are the simplest and the easiest in the world. However, the *haute école* rider in the circus also includes in the programme certain acrobatic feats such as making the horse rear, kneel, and jump over lighted candelabras placed on a table, dance, and waltz. Comparing pure *haute école* and *haute école* as practiced in the circus, General Decarpentry says that it is "of no concern to the circus rider if a few connoisseurs, enlightened by their equestrian education, are saddened

Horses at liberty.

by the perversion of their art as displayed in his presentations... The circus rider must arouse the enthusiasm of the Philistines by his stunts, acrobatics, and airs of bravura. Extravagance of movements, sometimes even frenzy, is necessary to enchant the audience, rather than purity of style. While Baucher had real talent, he was forced, as General L'Hotte put it, 'to sacrifice to false gods.'"[26]

Interesting is what Victor Franconi, a circus rider of *haute école* and other types of equestrian activities, says about *haute école* as practiced in the circus. In a letter to Baron de Vaux and presented in *Écuyers et Ecuyères,* Victor Franconi says:

[Circus] equitation is the same as it has been practiced in the old schools and as practiced in the modern ones. The *manège* airs are the same; nothing has been invented, unless one refers to the circus which, I believe, makes one think of equestrian eccentricities: the Spanish walk, the Spanish trot, the horse executing the passage (see note), his forelegs lengthened, or the crossing of forelegs or hind legs, and many other movements, movements that have never been part of *haute école* strictly speaking. It is true that the former *écuyers* could match these tricks, pardon the expression, against the high airs, almost all having been abandoned for quite some time, namely, the croupades, ballotades, lançades, courbettes, etc.[27]

26   General Decarpentry, *Academic Equitation*, London: J.A. Allen, 1971, 3.
27   Baron de Vaux, *Écuyers et Ecuyères*, Paris: J. Rothschild, 1893, 2. It should

Franconi then goes on to explain that performing *haute école* in the circus presents certain difficulties due to the circular shape of the ring, difficulties that do not arise in a *manège* that is shaped as a rectangle, for there the horse's equilibrium remains regular. To counteract the centrifugal force in a ring, the horse never places his four limbs with equal force on the ground. To prevent himself from being thrown out of the ring, the horse places his weight principally on his bipeds on the inner part of the circle. Since the center of the ring is slightly less elevated, it results in the horse's equilibrium being compromised. This sometimes makes a horse appear as though he is limping. And, Franconi adds, to make certain that a horse does not limp, it is necessary to have him move occasionally on a straight line.

Franconi also states that during the period of dressage, the horse's haunches often resist the rassembler by throwing themselves to the right and to the left; sometimes, even after the horse has been trained, the strains and stresses on the hindquarters persist, due to weakness or pain, thus making the rassembler difficult for him.

While Franconi mentions some of the difficulties that arise in the training of the horse and the consequences resulting from the horse's performance in the ring, and mentions some of the "eccentricities" as practiced in the circus, he does not refer to the fact, the main one it seems to me, that the circus rider must please and titillate the spectator and perform with greater movement and dramatic show, even frenzy, as Decarpentry puts it, than is necessary.

Sometimes variations of *haute école* were performed when an *ecuyère* on horseback executed movements of *haute école* and was followed by a dancer imitating on foot the movements of the horse. Sometimes two *ecuyères* or an *écuyer* and *ecuyère* performed a double *haute école* programme, as did Elise Petzold and Emilie Loisset in the Cirque Loisset and the Circus Renz.

---

be noted that in circus language "passage" means a horse moving sideways; in dressage competition "passage" means a slow, elevated trot.

Pour moì, l'ecuyère en la plenitude de ses moyens est supérieure à toutesles gloires du chant, de la danse et de l'art dramatique, à une Cinté-Damoreau ou à une Déjazet, à une Taglioni ou à une Dorual.
(Honoré de Balzac)

For me, the ecuyère, in full control of her talents, is superior to all the glories of song, dance and dramatic art, superior to a Cinté-Damoreau or to a Déjazet, to a Taglioni, or to a Dorval. (Famous actresses and dancers of the period.)

CHAPTER III:
THE ECUYERE IS QUEEN IN THE CIRCUS

While many *écuyers* of the nineteenth century, *écuyers* such as Laurent Franconi, François Baucher, Victor Franconi, James Fillis, de Corbie, and many others, were greatly admired, it was the *ecuyères* who began to dominate the scene in popularity and talent, beginning in the late eighteen thirties with Caroline Loyo and ending around the late eighteen eighties. This is especially true with respect to *haute école*. As Thétard points out, "it was during the great period of the circus, from the eighteen forties to the end of the century, that the *ecuyère* was the queen of the ring."[28] In her elegant attire, the *amazone collant*, which showed off her splendid figure, she represented the feminine ideal of that period, a period that admired the feminine form and made the dandies and sportsmen stand in the area between stall and *manège* to get a close glimpse of the *ecuyères* as they entered the ring. It was the *ecuyère* who gave distinction and, undoubtedly, sex appeal to the circus.

In *Écuyers et Ecuyères* Vaux says:

"Merely a few years ago, l'équitation de *haute école* was the exclusive privilege of the *écuyer*; to him alone belonged the knowledge of making a horse execute all the airs of *manège* familiar to us today: the *rassembler*,

---

28 Henry Thétard, *La Merveilleuse Histoire du cirque*, Vol I, 194.

determining the horse's equilibrium, using the aids with finesse and tact, and the development of the artificial aids, all were the prerogatives of the strong sex. However, very recently, woman (always curious) made her appearance; she took her role seriously and, under the tutelage and direction of famous professors of equitation, she succeeded in putting herself forward and in making use of the horse as well as could any man.

I will say that even greater obstacles face the *ecuyère*. In order to train the school horse, the *écuyer* has the use of his two legs and his two hands; due to the conformation of the saddle and her position at the left shoulder of the horse, the *ecuyère* has only her left leg as aid, and, to direct her horse, she has only her left hand, since the right hand is generally used to hold her crop. And yet, all these difficulties have been overcome on the part of a number of *ecuyères* by means of feel or tact."[29]

By equestrian tact is meant the use of discretion, finesse, sensitivity on the part of trainer/rider for a horse's disposition, his way of reacting. It means the use of judgement but also a certain amount of instinct which enables the rider to evaluate the most subtle movements of the horse, determine the use and strength of the aids, know when to stop with the execution of a particular movement, how long to train, when to punish or praise. Thus equestrian tact is that totality of attributes that an excellent horseman or horsewoman possesses and which distinguish him or her from merely a talented one. Of course, tremendous motivation is needed, together with physical stamina, energy, skill, and patience.

As will be noted in the sections dealing with the individual *ecuyères*, the reasons for becoming a professional *ecuyère* varied considerably. Anna Fillis, Emilie Loisset, Adelina Price, Elvira Guerra, the Jolibois-Cuzent sisters, belonged to circus families and received their training early in life, either as *ecuyère* de panneou performing equestrian acrobatics, or as *ecuyère de haute école*. Others had initially opted for other careers. Diane Dupont had first considered an acting career. Elise Petzold was so smitten by *haute école* in the circus that she went against her parents' wishes to become a good and obedient wife to someone chosen by her parents. However, even after her release from a convent to which the recalcitrant daughter had been sent, Elise still pined for a career as an *ecuyère* in the circus, forcing her parents to finally give in to her wishes. We know that Fanny Ghyga, who spent her childhood riding on her father's estate, was unhappily married and left home and husband to join an itinerant circus. Pauline Cuzent, first a musician, unable to join her sisters in equine acrobatics

29   Baron de Vaux, *Écuyers et Ecuyères*, 154-155.

due to a limp, was urged by François Baucher to become an *ecuyère* of *haute école* and offered to teach her. Motivated and taught by an excellent teacher, she became an excellent *ecuyère de haute école*. Jenny de Rhaden, who, early in life, had ridden with her father, became an *ecuyère* when her father, an invertebrate gambler, found himself penniless.

Many *ecuyères* not of circus lineage, believed that performing *haute école* in the circus would give them fame and fortune. Some may even have become *ecuyères* in the hope of finding a rich and important husband.

There were those, and there were many, who, when they became *haute école ecuyères*, or even before they became one, needed financial backing from other sources, an admirer perhaps, if financial backing from parental sources was not forthcoming. The *ecuyère haute école*, perhaps more so than the *ecuyère de panneau*, had to have considerable financial backing, at least initially, for she had to bring with her three trained horses, two trained in *haute école*, and one trained jumper. When Jenny de Rhaden's father became penniless, Jenny used the money she had inherited from her mother to buy the necessary horses.

Furthermore, the upkeep of these horses required considerable finances. And if one of the horses became ill or died, another horse had to be acquired and, even if already trained in *haute école* movements and airs, working together was of paramount importance and required time for, once again, that special harmony between horse and rider had to be established. That was the lot of the equestrian artist, for the loss of a horse was overwhelming as compared to, say, the sculptor, the musician, or the painter, for whom the loss of tools could be readily replaced.

The life of these *ecuyères* was not as glamorous as it had seemed to them initially and as it seemed to the public. In her autobiography, Jenny de Rhaden mentions many unpleasant incidents that occurred, despite the fact that she was accompanied by her father and aunt, later by her husband. Sportsmen who were frequenters of the circus often tried to take advantage of an *ecuyère* performing in the circus; one admirer of Jenny de Rhaden, after being rebuked, said that, after all, it was merely a matter of pursuing an artist. Directors often took advantage of an *ecuyère*'s financial problems, as, for example, when Director Salamonsky took possession of Jenny de Rhaden's outstanding jumper by means of a subterfuge, or when an *ecuyère* was sent to the lesser branch of a circus in order not to compete with the director's wife or daughter. In her autobiography, Rhaden says:

."..the career of an *ecuyère de haute école* merely has an exterior luster. These deceptive appearances soon lose their glitter when one begins to consider them more closely, and when one looks backstage and investigates seriously..."[30]

The sad endings of some of the glamorous, talented, and successful *ecuyères* are too numerous for one not to see a pattern. Emilie Loisset was crushed to death by her horse at the age of twenty-six while performing at the Cirque d'Hiver during her final engagement, just before her planned marriage to the Prince von Hatzfeld. Fanny Ghyga fell off her horse and was dragged through the vast arena of the Hippodrome, and died a few days later when gangrene set in. Jenny de Rhaden suddenly' became blind and, despite her condition, was talked by the director into performing on her already blind horse. Caroline Loyo died poor and forgotten amidst her mementos. The greatly admired and talented Pauline Cuzent died before she reached forty, lonely and poor; she most likely died of tuberculosis. Antoinette Cuzent-Lejars, who had charmed Europe with her passion and daring equestrian acrobatics, reached old age but also poverty. She eked out a living working in pantomimes playing minor roles, even serving as usher in the circus where she had once been so triumphant. A similar fate awaited Mathilde Monnet. In her old age she was forced to sell different kinds of riding whips along the boulevards of Paris to earn a living. She then became cashier at the Cirque Fernando. A sad ending for a much applauded *ecuyère*.

Some *ecuyères* did succeed when they left the circus. Elise Petzold became Madame de la Blanchère. We hear of her again in the early 1930s at the age of eighty. Clotilde Loisset, unlike her sister Emilie, married her prince.

Hughes Le Roux observes that:

...there are two very different kinds of *ecuyères* of *haute école*, first the wives, daughters, and sisters of circus directors...Sometimes these directors hope to marry their daughters into bourgeois families—or even princely ones—but hesitate to exhibit their daughters semi-clad as it might frighten off potential husbands.[31]

In a Preface to Vaux's *Écuyers et Ecuyères*, there are two amusing letters presented by Henri Meilhac, writer of popular plays,

---

30 Baronne Jenny de Rhaden, Autobiographic, *Roman d'une Ecuyère*, Paris: Charles Eitel, ed. 1902, 90.

31 Hughes Le Roux, *Les Jeux du Cirque et la vie foraine*, 128.

that touch on *ecuyères* and marriage. Among his many mementos, Meilhac found two letters he had saved, one written by a Madame Potiquet, whose daughter had reached the marriageable age, to Madame la Comtesse Soperani, a former *ecuyère*, and the Comtesse's reply. These two letters present, in a sense, Meilhac's opinion of *ecuyères* in general. When Vaux had asked Meilhac to write a preface to his book *Écuyers et Ecuyères*, he felt that the two letters."..seemed to him to be exactly what this preface should be."[32]

Madame Potiquet's problem, outlined in her letter, was that she had a daughter, Emma, of almost seventeen years of age, an age that forces a mother of that period to think seriously of the future of her daughter. Naturally, she wanted her daughter to marry well and become rich and happy, that she would one day have her hotel particulier, diamonds, horses. But she wanted her Emma to get these things honestly, that is, honestly. Monsieur Potiquet shared her wishes. He was, after all, a virtuous bourgeois.

Madame Potiquet recounts how one evening she, her husband, and Emma's godfather, Monsieur Frangipan, had a family counsel. First Monsieur Potiquet had his say, then Madame Potiquet had her say. Monsieur Frangipan said nothing. All he did was drink one little glass after another. Finally, after several glasses, he said:

"The question is simple: You want your little one to remain a good girl, and, while remaining a good girl, she can, nevertheless, obtain all the things that those dream of who do not remain good girls... "

Both Monsieur and Madame Potiquet replied simultaneously "exactly."

"Well" said Monsieur Frangipan, "have her make her debut in the circus."

At that point Monsieur Potiquet objected. After all, as a good and virtuous bourgeois he did not, as he put it, want to see his daughter standing on a horse, showing her legs in public.

"Nobody is speaking of that. Have her make her debut as an écuyère de *haute école*` stated Monsieur Frangipan,."..we are not talking of the theatre or the cafe-concert... The work of an *ecuyère* is very proper and distinguished. Neither is it very difficult, for the horse generally knows what he must do and asks nothing of the person who rides him, except that he not be contradicted during and after his exercises. An *ecuyère* is loudly applauded by what is the best in

---

32   Vaux, *Écuyers et Ecuyères*, X. The following quotations are taken from the Preface by Meilhac which deals with the two letters.

Parisian high society and in foreign countries. As far as lovers are concerned, for in the circus as in the Opera, there are lovers, but they are lovers of a special kind, for never will they allow themselves to speak of love without immediately speaking of marriage. A man who adores and courts an *ecuyère* without intending to marry her, would despise himself, and one knows that for a gallant man there is nothing worse than to despise oneself. One other thing of note, all the adorers in the wings of the circus were princes, or at least archiducs."

The discussion ceased when Emma returned home from her friend's party. Monsieur Frangipan swallowed a last little glass, Emma said goodnight to all, and retired.

That night, in bed, Monsieur and Madame Potiquet found the suggestion made by Monsieur Frangipan fine, but wondered if it were true; it was, after all, too good to be true.

Suddenly Madame Potiquet let out a cry, for she remembered that Madame la Comtesse had traveled in the world of circuses, that she had made her debut as an *ecuyère de haute école* and that after having had a rapid and brilliant career, had married Monsieur le Comte. She decided to write to her for help.

At some stage of her letter writing, Madame Potiquet referred to the fact that her husband was looking over her shoulder to see what she was writing and was questioning her wisdom in reminding Madame la Comtesse that she had once been an *ecuyère*. Madame Potiquet told Monsieur Potiquet to leave her alone and that Madame la Comtesse would be only too willing to help a mother who wished the best for her daughter's future, especially as she wanted her daughter to succeed honestly. She hoped that Madame la Comtesse would advise her, honestly and truthfully, without exaggerating, "like the good Comtesse that you are." She signed off "with the profoundest respect, your humble and devoted servant, cousin of the famous Madame Cardinal."

Indeed, the good Comtesse Soperani did answer Madame Potiquet's letter saying that "I will not hide the fact that I take great pleasure in answering, especially as it gives me the possibility of looking back at my whole life."

Already at an early age Madame la Comtesse had wanted to be an *ecuyère de haute école* "I was one... yes, and by and large, I was one, and the Comte married me because I was one."

Madame la Comtesse remembered how Monsieur Cardinale had just bought a new hat. When the future Madame la Comtesse saw this hat, the idea came to her to try it on. Madame Cardinale (known to both Mesdames Potiquet and Picou) gave a cry of admiration at the sight of the twelve year old wearing her husband's hat. It was then that the destiny of the little girl was sealed. "It was impossible," wrote the Comtesse, "to imagine anything prettier than me with that hat."

Later, as a young girl, there was no need to have a family counsel, since she wanted to make her entry into the world with such a hat on her head, a man's hat—an *haut-de-forme*. She had attended the circus, the Hippodrome, and had seen many *ecuyères* riding magnificent horses executing the most audacious pirouettes. She heard people applaud them, loudly and repeatedly, making the *ecuyères* return again and again to take more salutes and bows. The applause and the hat had gone to Pauline's head. She then and there decided to become an *ecuyère* of *haute école*. The mother of the future Comtesse, Madame Picou, whose only thought was the happiness of her darling daughter, consented immediately.

They marched to the best tailor to have the *amazone* attire made. When Pauline tried it on for the first time, Madame Picou fainted, but not completely. She was still capable of taking her daughter by the hand and going together to a photographer. The best, of course. The photographer took the daughter's photograph. It was a masterpiece. Even Madame Picou admitted that the photograph was even better than the original model, although the original was not bad either. The photographer made thousands of copies and inundated Paris with them, stating that it represented Mademoiselle X, *ecuyère haute école*. The photograph was seen everywhere and she was already famous, as a horsewoman, although she still did not know how to get on a horse or stay on one. She became so famous that people wanted to know who was Mlle. X. Some even managed to find out. Pauline received many letters and many visits. One day, alone in the house, the concierge brought in a visiting card from a certain Monsieur François Chenu. No sooner had she read the name, when Monsieur Chenu made his appearance. He told her that he, too, was a horseman and, as such, wished to make her acquaintance. He spoke of his love for her in such a way that she realized that as an *ecuyère* something was missing, and that something was a crop. Not having a crop, she mustered as much indignation and virtue as she could. Monsieur Chenu had sufficient intelligence to depart from the scene. Such was the first communication of the future Madame la Comtesse with her future husband. She perceived that Monsieur Chenu was a timid, decent man, very much in love.

Meanwhile, with a letter of introduction in hand, the future *ecuyère* and her mother went to see the director of a circus. He received them graciously, for he had already seen the photograph of

Mademoiselle X. When he was made aware that the girl wanted to be an *ecuyère*, the director asked if she had already been on a horse.

"Yes," answered the mother, "once at Montmorency when she was very young, but I'm not sure that counts."

"No, that does not count" answered the director.

He then advised them that the daughter take riding lessons, gave them the name of a *manège*, and told them to return in two or three years. "Then we'll see what we can do," he added.

Both were quite astonished, not to say disappointed, that it would take so long to learn to ride. They went to the *manège* the director had indicated and the future *ecuyère* and Comtesse began her first lesson. She had motivation, energy, but her disposition as a horsewoman did not indicate that she was exceptionally talented. After each lesson the *écuyer* in charge of her training, made a little grimace.

"It's not yet quite that," he said, "but it'll come, it'll come." On occasion mother and daughter went to the circus to see the director who gave them tickets for the evening performance. On one occasion, the daughter was invited to go backstage to familiarize herself with those who might later become her colleagues. And it was then that she came once more face to face with François Chenu. He indicated that he was even more in love with her than ever; he was hardly more polite now than at their first meeting. And he failed to follow the famous rule, as Monsieur Frangipan had indicated, that in the wings of the circus, a man who pronounces the word "love" must immediately add the word "marriage." He then declared that he would have Pauline, that in the final analysis, he would end up having her, regardless of the means. He offered to place at her feet his entire fortune.

Pauline also noticed that Chenu was limping very pronouncedly. He admitted that very morning during a ride in the Bois, he had fallen from his horse. This made Pauline look at him with interest. She noticed that he had rounded thighs and that he most likely sat on a horse like an orange on a plate. Pauline left him saying that she hoped he had better luck the next time he got on a horse. As far as his proposals were concerned, she dealt with them with all the necessary pride and virtue.

The lessons continued and soon mother and daughter were told that Pauline could now become an *ecuyère*. The mother was not rich, neither was she poor, and when she was told that an *ecuyère* had to have two or three horses trained in *haute école* and that each horse would cost about 6,000 francs, the mother did not hesitate. And so the horses were purchased. They were beautiful horses. One was especially beautiful. He was called Crocodile. And the *écuyer* who was Pauline's teacher taught Crocodile to execute wonderful movements with the most imperceptible indications. Crocodile did the Spanish walk, he turned, did voltes, danced, went down on his knees, went around the ring, his two front legs on the ring curb. All Pauline had to do was adjust her movements to the horse's movements. With the help of her *écuyer*, Pauline learned to do what was necessary to make the horse execute the many movements he had been taught. And it was agreed that she and her horse would go to the circus and undergo a general test. The press was not invited, but the director was kind enough to attend. The mother had invited several friends to attend. Crocodile and Pauline, one carrying the other, somehow managed to get through the trial with success. However, the director said that it was impossible to take her on at the moment, but if she wanted to make her debut in Madrid, he would see to it that she got an engagement in Spain.

Off went mother, daughter, Crocodile and his two companions, plus a neighbor who had never been to Spain and wanted to take advantage of the situation. They did not take along with them the *écuyer*, which, they soon realized, was a big mistake.

Huge posters announced Pauline's appearance: "Mademoiselle Pauline will appear on her horse Crocodile." That very day Pauline read in a French newspaper that a French sportsman, Monsieur Paul [François] C., had, in a hunt, just been the victim of a rather serious accident. So, the orange had not been able to remain on the plate.

The moment of Pauline's presentation arrived. She received a thunderous applause as she entered the ring, but it was the applause for the sight of a pretty woman, and it was the only applause she got. Aware that he no longer had his trainer beside him, Crocodile behaved in a most disastrous manner. When Pauline asked him to go forwards, he went backwards, instead of kneeling, he sat down, when asked to do the Spanish walk, he did something...indescribable. Spain was angry. And, added the future Madame la Comtesse in her letter to Madame Potiquet, "this was the sum total of my rapid and brilliant career."

Pauline's mother became ill. They returned to Paris where, a few months later, she died. Pauline received a polite letter from Chenu, then a few more. In each one he repeated that he wanted her, and that he would have her, making a number of offers. A year later, somewhat poorer, as the money her mother had left her was beginning to dwindle, she sold Crocodile and the two other horses. She pondered a great deal about her fate. She had no talent. She was not even a good horsewoman, but still, that was what she could do best, which was not much. She returned to the initial director who told her that he needed someone to ride in the Quadrille Louis XV. She accepted, although she was sorry that she could not wear the hat that suited her so well—the *haut-de-forme*. One day, backstage, she met Emilie Loisset who told her that the director was one of the best teachers she had ever met, and Pauline hoped that one day she would benefit from his expertise.

The following day Pauline appeared in the quadrille. What happened during that performance appeared in all the newspapers. It was her turn to move. She tapped her horse with her crop. He refused to advance. She gave a second tap, somewhat firmer. The horse slipped on his hind legs, toppled over the ring curb, and horse and rider fell into the first rows of spectators. There were screams, Pauline received a blow on her head, and fainted. When she regained consciousness, she found herself in her apartment with François Chenu at her side. He was leaning on two canes, looking at her with kindness.

"Just imagine," he said to her, "is there an animal more stupid than the horse. When he doesn't throw you to the ground, he manages to fall on top of you." He then looked at her penetratingly and asked: "Must I marry you in order to have you? Is no other way possible?"

Pauline made a vague gesture with her head.

"Well then" sighed François, "so be it. I shall marry you. One can marry you now that you are all alone in the world."

This sounded like an unfavorable reference to her mother and Pauline became furious.

"After all," said Pauline, "the name Chenu is not so wonderful and there is no reason to be so haughty."

François laughed. "If the name does not meet with your approval, we can take another one, our means allow it."

So he bought the title of a Roman Comte. Pauline became a Comtesse. Madame la Comtesse concluded her letter to Madame Potiquet, saying that,

Indeed the function of an *ecuyère de haute école* is not always that of a mechanical doll on a mechanical horse. Rather, it is an art and those who are able to surmount all the difficulties deserve to achieve fame and fortune. But to overcome these difficulties time is needed, a great deal of time, at least eight or ten years. Furthermore, it is necessary to have the requisite attributes that not everyone possesses, and I can, indeed, vouch for that. It is necessary that the *ecuyère de haute école* start out when very young, that she be a child first playing with a ball, then begin to jump through hoops, and vault... But then, with all this behind them, how many, since 1870, can one name who have become famous? Perhaps a dozen at the most. And even then, among the five or six, there are degrees of fame.

Madame la Comtesse said that she tried to be honest in her letter to Madame Potiquet, suggesting that the daughter be satisfied finding happiness on foot. Training horses is fine, but it is not bad at all to train a husband, as Madame la Comtesse had done. Actually, added Madame la Comtesse, "the Count is not too unhappy as he reads over my shoulder and kisses me to thank me for the last sentence.— Oh, I forgot... I obtained from my husband the promise that he would never get on a horse. To make him keep this promise I, too, promised never to ride again."

Quite obviously, these two rather long letters I have paraphrased are facetious letters and Meilhac, the playwright, is having fun at the expense of *ecuyères* in general. But he is also warning future *ecuyères* that much hard work must be expended in order to achieve success, that talent, innate and learned, and motivation are necessary, and, perhaps, a little bit of luck. Too many young women, hearing the applause that some *ecuyères* were getting, and perhaps hearing that some were even receiving great marriage proposals, thought that a pretty face and a good figure, rendered even better in an *amazone* co¡lant, plus a few lessons on a horse, would bring all these wondrous things within easy reach.

Physical exercise will have the same fortifying influence on French society that it had on English society. (Baron de Vaux)

CHAPTER IV:
WOMEN AND SPORTS

Much has been said of the supremacy of the *ecuyère* in the circus in the nineteenth century and that, in more ways than one, she and the *écuyer* had preserved *haute école* at a time when Classical or savant riding was disappearing and was being replaced by outdoor riding.

It is important to note that this was also the period when books were appearing dealing with women and equestrian matters. In 1817 appeared Jules Pellier's *La Selle et le Costume* de *l'Amazone*. That same year also saw the appearance of L. de Pons d'Hostrum's *L'Écuyer des Dames ou Lettre sur l'Equitation.* In 1842 P.- A. Aubert published *L'Equitation des Dames.* In 1852 appeared A. Roger's *Le Livre d'Equitation des Dames.* In 1861 Victor Franconi's *La Cavalière* was published. That same year appeared, in French, Stirling-Clarke's *Le Cheval et l'Amazone* and her *Guide d'équitation pour les dames.* In 1888 *L'Amazone—au manège—à la promenade* by F. Musany appeared, as did le Comte de Montigny's *L'Equitation des dames.*

Thus not only was the *ecuyère* queen in the circus for a number of decades, manuals on equitation were being written for and about her, and for and about horsewomen in general. In fact to be involved in horsemanship and other types of sports was becoming the thing to do. Sport activities were becoming respectable even for a woman. Why did this sudden interest in sports occur? What was happening in society that brought about these changes?

It is well-known that women have always ridden and it is assumed that many were taught how to ride, that is, they became horsewomen. But one is speaking here of the "grandes dames" who rode, sometimes astride, as they took part in a hunt, as did Diane de Poitiers and Anne de Beaujeu, or in battle as did Joan of Arc and Mathilda, Countess of Tuscany. In the Middle Ages, women rode to get from one place to the other and they used what is known as a sort of bench with a footrest, although in the *Canterbury Tales*, the woman of Bath rode like a man, and in the *Tristan* by Béroul, Iseut, rode "comme. un valet" (like a valet), that is, astride.

But as the nineteenth century progressed, it was no longer the *"grande dame,"* the aristocrat, who rode; the woman of the upper bourgeoisie also began to buy a horse and show herself in the Bois de Boulogne, accompanied by her spaniel or hound.

With an increasing interest in outdoor riding, interest in certain other sports began to make itself felt. According to Richard Holt in *Sport and Society in Modern France* little has been said by the social historian with respect to the rise of sports and the concomitant changes that were taking place in society in France as well as in England.

Indeed, the relationship between sport and society has been given little attention, that is, hardly any attempt has been made to show how sports move in step with certain changes taking place in society, changes such as democratization and the rise of leisure. And, it should be added, little has been said about the connection between women and sports and the place of women in society.

Men, that is, primarily men from the aristocracy, have always practiced certain kinds of physical skills, namely, the equestrian skills and the hunt, fencing and duelling, and shooting. With the onset of anglomania, democratization, and more leisure time, the bourgeoisie, upper and middle, began to emulate the aristocracy in terms of social prestige and fashion. The *"gentilhomme"* was being replaced by the "gentleman." Horsemanship, the hunt, fencing, pistol shooting became the thing to do for those who could afford these recreational activities. Soon other recreational activities began to be introduced into France, namely, football and rugby; gymnastics and running, activities practiced in Classical antiquity, began to be re-introduced. Even the middle and petite bourgeoisie began to show an interest in certain sports. This is a considerable change in attitude on the part of the French, since the French, especially the bourgeoisie, were not considered to be enthusiasts of sports at least at that time.

What is especially interesting is that the country that had made so little of sport at the time was the country that attempted to re-introduce the Olympic Games. For the man responsible for the reinvention of amateur international competition was a French aristocrat, le Baron Pierre de Coubertin. Unfortunately, Coubertin was ignored in France, as he was elsewhere, to the extent that, according to Eugen Weber, he was not even mentioned in the pages of the *Petit Larousse* or the *Encyclopedia Britannica*. One important factor with respect to Coubertin's failure regarding the introduction of physical education among French youth was that he was primarily concerned with the education of the elite. To make sportsmen out of young Frenchmen of the bourgeoisie, where the idea of organized athletics,

Dressing up for fun. A plate which appears in the book by J.G. Prizeluis "*Etwas für Liebhaberinnen der Reiterey*" (Something for those women who like riding), Leipzig, Weidmann, 1777. Note the astride seat which Prizeluis favored for women. Most likely a portrait of Princess Helena Charlotte to whom the book is dedicated.

An *amazone* in a *manège* doing the passage. Painting by Edmond Grandjean.

especially team games as they were practiced in England, with the notion of fair play, respect for the rules of the game, was still unheard of.

Not to be outdone, women of the aristocracy and the bourgeoisie very soon began to show a keen interest in sports, that is, in physical recreation. In addition to horsemanship, fencing, pistol shooting, tennis, falconry on horseback, archery, swimming, and gymnastics were also practiced. While the writer Catulle-Mendès accepts equitation as a sport for women, he becomes rather ironic in his preface to Vaux' *Les Femmes de Sport* published in 1885. In his discussion of women indulging in sports, especially the more violent ones, Mendès says that woman, once this frail creature who needed protection, now no longer needs the protection of men, be they husband or a "less legitimate companion." And, bemoans Mendès, "Alas, men forlorn and sad, now rendered useless."[33]

In *Les Femmes de Sport,* Baron de Vaux makes the following observation:

Influenced for the past twenty-five years by English customs, the condition of women in France has undergone important modifications. Sport, with all the changes that it has brought with it, is now an integral part of the life of our mondaines, that is, the sophisticates. In the past, the dance and, by way of exception, equitation, were the only physical exercises included in the program of feminine education. It was not even considered proper for a woman to indulge in sport.... How all that has changed today![34]

And, Vaux continues:

Gymnastics and everything linked to sport, in the water or on dry land, is now allowed to make an entrance in the most austere houses. Horse racing and equestrian competition have developed in woman a taste for equitation. In the last war (the Franco-Prussian War) she became accustomed to the odor of gunpowder, so much so that she now shoots hares and rabbits... And finally, the increasing interest in the art of fencing... has given her the desire to handle the fencing foil...[35]

And just as Coubertin believed that the practice of different

---

33 Baron de Vaux, *Les Femmes de Sports*, Paris: C. Marpon et E. Flammarion, 1885, IV.

34 Ibid., 1-2.

35 Ibid., 2.

sports was good for one's health and moral fiber, so, too, did Vaux believe in the efficacy of sports. "No doubt," says Vaux, "physical exercise will have the same fortifying influence on French society that it had on English society."[36]

In this atmosphere of rising, yet restrained, physical activities, of special interest is the introduction of the velocipede which became increasingly popular as the century entered the period known as the belie époque. The new men of the petite bourgeoisie, young clerks working in banks, insurance companies, and the newly established department stores, found a new sense of freedom and relaxation in the velocipede from routine office work.

In fact, the velocipede, not mentioned by Vaux, is perhaps of special interest with respect to the changes that were taking place in the life of women, for with its advent, they began to assert themselves more forcefully. Donning bloomers, women began to enjoy the freedom to travel leisurely in the countryside and the delights of solitude. The numerous posters done by well-known artists such as Toulouse-Lautrec, depict women riding on a velocipede in the countryside or in a *manège*, sometimes alone, sometimes with companions. This sense of freedom that women felt with respect to the advent of the velocipede had a similar impact on women on horseback. But since to maintain a horse required more money and leisure, riding on horseback was limited to those who could afford it.

It was only in the nineteenth century that women began to be recognized for their equestrian skills, whether outdoors or in a *manège*, whether as *ecuyère* or as amateur horsewoman. This was one of the reasons why Ernest Molier established his circus for his friends and acquaintances enabling men, and especially women, to demonstrate their skills in a number of equestrian fields and different types of acrobatics. It was also in the nineteenth century that the terms *amazone* and *ecuyère* began to be used. Ernest Molier distinguishes between the two terms in *L'Equitation et le cheval*. The term *amazone* refers to "the woman who rides for the pleasure of sport and does outdoor equitation, that is, who rides in the Bois de Boulogne, or rides to hounds"; an *ecuyère* "is a women who specializes in *haute école*."[37] And, to this latter definition, one should include women such as Blanche Allarty or Antoinette Cuzent-Lejars, who also vaulted and did acrobatics on horseback and deserve the name of *ecuyère*. Furthermore, many *ecuyères* of *haute école* also became *amazones*, as defined by Molier,

---
36 Ibíd.,3-4.
37 Ernest Molier, *L'Equitation et le Cheval*, Paris: Pierre Lafitte, 1911, 287.

since they also enjoyed riding in the countryside or in the woods with enterprising vigor or even at breakneck speeds.

As noted earlier, Classical or equitation savante, generally speaking, began to be an activity of the past. And it is ironic that Classical riding was expressing itself and, in a sense, being preserved, in the circus, the very place that was looked upon with scorn by the Classical purists, the former *écuyer*s and teachers at the Ecole de Versailles, the very men who refused to consider that which was being practiced in the circus as Classical equitation or *haute école*. Even more ironic is the fact that with the closing of the doors of the Ecole de Versailles in 1830, many of the men who had been schooled in Classical or savant riding, moved to Paris to teach the dandies and the *amazones* the new and different way of riding, namely exterior riding. Alas, the same attitude is sometimes evident today, especially in the United States, on the part of many dressage riders who perform *haute école* competitively, expressing a certain amount of contempt for horsemen and horsewomen who perform *haute école* dressed in costumes of days gone by. "Circusy" is the epithet they use. The great Mestro Nuno Oliveira often dressed in the age of Pluvinel or La Guérinière when performing *haute école*. There are photographs of him sitting majestically on a centuries-old type of horse, the Iberian horse, doing all the *haute école* airs as defined by La Guérinière, and wearing the dress of the eighteenth century aristocrat, wig included. According to Dominique Jando, Oliveira also appeared on special occasions in circus rings, notably that of the Cirque d'Hiver.

Women of the aristocracy and bourgeoisie frequented the fashionable *manège*s run by Comte d'Aure, Jules Pellier, P.A. Aubert, F. Musany, and many others, who, to earn a living, had to be fashionable and teach their pupils the new equitation—outdoor equitation. Some, like Jules Pellier, did continue to teach the old method, that is, the movements of *haute école*.

A wealth of paintings portray women on horseback, singly or accompanied by other women, children, or men. Or else they are portrayed in a *manège* executing a collected walk, the School walk, or the Spanish walk. The best known painters of *ecuyères* and horses were Alfred de Dreux and Edmond Grandjean who painted portraits of many of the *ecuyères* of the period. To these painters one must also include artists such as Renoir, Toulouse-Lautrec, Degas, Seurat and many others who have, through their art, rendered the nineteenth century, especially the second half, the age of the horse, the age of the *ecuyère*, and the age of the circus.

CHAPTER V:
CAROLINE LOYO, PAULINE CUZENT, LABELLE MADAME LEJARS AND THE CUZENT / LEJARS COMPANY

CAROLINE LOYO

While Caroline Loyo was considered one of the first and most important *écuyères de haute école* during the first half of the nineteenth century, mention should be made of at least two names, namely Philippine Tourniaire and Constance Chiarini.

Philippine Tourniaire was the wife of a travelling circus director, Jacques Tourniaire who, after working for Philip Astley and Laurent Franconi, formed his own circus company in 1801 where his young wife, in *amazone* attire, presented horses executing *haute école* movements. Constance Chiarini, as indicated earlier, belonged to the famous Chiarini family. As so often happens, some outstanding artists or performers are forgotten, others remembered. This also happened to Virginie Kenebel, Victor Franconi's wife, who, while an outstanding *ecuyère de panneau*, has been remembered only *en passant*.

Caroline Loyo made her debut at the Cirque Olympique around 1833 at the age of seventeen, having left her home one day together with her black horse. "Black was her horse, black were her eyes,"[38] said Jules Janin, writer and critic, and enthusiast of the circus during this period. It did not take long for the "diva of the cravache" (the diva of the crop) to make a name for herself in *haute école* at the Cirque Olympique and at the Cirque des Champs-Elysées. While having had some experience in horsemanship before she arrived in Paris with her horse, she received instruction from Jules-Charles Pellier and, later, from François Baucher who, with Laurent Franconi, ran the shortlived circus in Le Pecq, a suburb of Paris.

Loyo was pretty and vivacious, with a good figure and looked very striking on her horse. She also liked to dress in different flowing costumes with flowing hair. She immediately became the rage of Paris. All the sportsmen and horsemen, members of the Jockey Club, popular painters and artists, and the young rakes pressed into the gangways and corridors to see Loyo and applaud her just before she entered the ring. When Baucher began to perform at the Cirque des

---

38   Baron de Vaux, *Écuyers et Ecuyères*, 109.

Champs-Elysées, Loyo shared the prestigious last position with him on alternate evenings. It is said that Baucher wanted Pauline Cuzent to rival Loyo in *haute école* riding and if Pauline did not surpass Caroline, she certainly became her equal and friendly rival. The problem in attempting to compare the two *ecuyères* and preferring the temperament, looks, and performance of one over the other, is mainly a matter of personal taste. Caroline was aggressive and executed everything con brio; Pauline was quiet, yet strong, always the lady.

Loyo had several excellent horses, Mamouth, Jupiter, Junon, Rutler, and Russe, whom she trained herself. To some critics, she was a severe trainer, demanding total discipline from her horses. She is supposed to have said: "I will work to the death (*je crèverai*) every horse who resists."[39] It is also known that she did not ride only well-trained horses, but also horses which were barely broken.

Loyo executed all the movements of *haute école* with a certain amount of brio which certainly thrilled both uninformed spectators and the knowledgeable horsemen. Jules Janin, writing for the *Journal des Débats* on 9 August 1841, had this to say of Loyo:

Alas, I have seen many a young girl fall! Mile Caroline alone, so far, in this brilliant milling of pink crops and golden stirrup irons, has not made a single false step. Until now, the circus has been gentle and favorable to her. She has gone from Charybdis to Scylla, (from exoticism to provincialism) without losing a single flock of her dress of snow. But also, how learned she is, what a terrifying *écuyer*! Is this actually a woman? Unquestionably, for she has the grace, the figure, the glance, the dainty foot, the long hair of a woman. She is not playing a part, this woman puts into her performance all the seriousness she can muster. She does not perform acrobatics on her horse, she rides her horse. Neither does she choose to ride four-legged comedians of the circus. What she needs is a veritable horse of flesh and blood. She says that a horse for her is like a rime for a poet, a slave who must obey.

And look at this passage on Rutler: Rutler is being stubborn, he is in a bad mood. Rutler, being an English thoroughbred, says to himself 'We actually won the battle of Waterloo,' humming to himself the ballad: 'No, no, they will not have the German Rhine' which always exasperated Rutler.

Caroline arrives. She takes hold of friend Rutler unceremoniously. And then she jumps up in the saddle. There, that's

---

39   *Ibid.*, 114.

Caroline Loyo on Junon, most likely a sketch by Alfred de Dreux.

done. Right away the animal rears and bounds forward. He defends himself, he rages, he is furious. Then he dances to the tune of this ballad.

'Ah! We will not have the German Rhine?' repeats Caroline. 'Well, take this for the German Rhine, take this for Waterloo, take this for Wellington, and that's for you.' Meanwhile, they waltz, gallop, and piaffe. 'Stand up now, and if you resist once more I will place a napkin around your neck and you will have to dine with Monsieur Auriol.' They threw flowers at Caroline, I believe they even ended by throwing some at Rutler.

She's the equestrian Taglioni (famous ballerina), say some; she's Carlotta Grisi (famous dancer), say others.[40]

So wrote the aficionado Jules Janin of Caroline Loyo.
Then the desire for greener pastures took hold of Caroline Loyo. She performed with the greatest success at the Circus Renz in Berlin. There she met François Loisset, a daring *écuyer*, whom she married in 1852. She was especially acclaimed in England where the circus became the meeting place of all the gentry.

---

40   *Ibid.*, 109-110.

They went to see Loyo as they went to see Adelina Patti, the famous Italian opera singer who graced the Opera de Paris.
Vaux recounts an incident that occurred in London one night. "It was raining torrents and Loyo had no cab to take her home. When the Duke of B. noticed her dilemma, he took her by the arm, while the Earl C. covered her with his cloak and accompanied her [Caroline Loyo] to the coach of Lord X.."[41]

Would these three aristocrats have been such gentlemen for a little ballet dancer or an actress? One can only speculate. After all, these aristocrats were, themselves, passionate and, perhaps, competent, horsemen and thus admired competent horsemanship in others, even in women. Their wives, sisters, daughters were, most likely, also competent horsewomen. Thus it is understandable that a talented horsewoman, even though performing in the circus, would be treated with a certain amount of respect.

After a successful tour in the capitals of Europe, Loyo returned to Paris in 1846 and continued to perform at the various circuses, the Cirque National (which a few years later became the Cirque d'Hiver) as well as at the Hippodrome.

Usually, the *écuyer*s and *ecuyères* kept their horses in the stalls that belonged to the circus where they were performing. But Caroline had placed her horses with her former instructor, Pellier. Every morning Loyo came to Pellier's *manège* to work her horses. All were beautiful and beautifully trained and disciplined. While she had acquired a few new horses, Rutler, Junon, and Jupiter were still with her. She preferred to board her horses with Pellier where she felt she was able to deal with them in the way and when she wanted. She even groomed them herself and gave them all the care that a knowledgeable horseman would have given. This was unusual for a woman to do and it may explain why she was so successful with her horses and why they were so disciplined. Since she could not exercise all her horses every day, she worked them regularly in hand, making them piaffe, passage, or Spanish walk, or she worked them on the lunge at the trot or canter. The horses she could not ride herself, she had the young pupils of Pellier lead for short walks; she saw to it that all got some exercise.

In 1847, at the Hippodrome de l'Etoile she rode a mare. There, too, the press raved about her work on this newly acquired mount. Loyo's position was flawless, the use of her hands was gentle, yet forceful, making her horse execute movements with precision,

---

41   *Ibid.*, 111.

yet with grace. Her mare performed the piaffe and passage flawlessly. Because the Hippodrome had a large oval track, she was able to use the whole length and had her mare execute flying changes at one and at two tempi.

Louis Dejean, who was then the director of the Cirque Olympique and its summer annex the Cirque des Champs-Elysées, was displeased with her comment that she would work to death any horse who resisted her. To put her on the spot and, to some extent, to teach her a lesson, he asked her to ride a horse named Mahmoud, still wild and unbroken and who reared as soon as he saw a bit or even the shadow of a bit. Loyo got on Mahmoud; she had barely made the horse take a few steps when she succeeded, as Vaux puts it,

in making a lamb out of the lion... Poor Mahmoud! He allowed himself to be tamed by Caroline; he bent his proud head, he swept the Olympic dust with his flowing mane, he crawled before her; he crawled so much that she got rid of him right there. 'What do you want me to do with you, Mahmoud? I loved you because I was told that you could not support anything on your back, nothing on your head. You are too docile for me, you bore me.'[42]

Loyo was not only a rider of *haute école* working in a ring or a *manège*, like so many other circus *ecuyères*, she also liked to ride in the countryside, show off her mount and dog, and even race her horse. Vaux gives an account of Loyo racing two young dandies mounted on superb thoroughbreds.

Two young officers of the Ecole d'Etat-major were riding along the avenue Saint-Cloud with their horses at a slow canter. They were soon joined by two horsemen and a horsewoman who had their

---

42 *Ibid.*, 114, 115.

horses at a walk and were involved in a very animated discussion about which of their horses was the fastest, the horsewoman's little mare or the two thoroughbreds.

The two horsemen belonged to one of the famous houses and fortunes, their horses were beautiful English thoroughbreds. The *amazone* was Caroline Loyo on her mare, Junon, her preferred horse, and on whom she had great triumphs at the Cirque Olympique and the Cirque des Champs-Elysées.

Junon, a light *café-au-lait* mare, was greatly outshone by the two thoroughbreds. Even her conformation was not the best. But when ridden by Caroline, she was a marvel to behold, full of grace and energy.

The two young officers greeted the trio politely. To their surprise they were asked to slow down, told of the discussion the trio were having, and asked to serve as judges.

The owners of the thoroughbreds had questioned not only the value of Caroline's mare, but also her speed against the two thoroughbreds. The race.was on and it was decided that whoever first reached the oak which served as a marker to the roundabout, would be entertained at a supper at the Moulin-Rouge by the losers. The distance between the oak and the five riders was approximately six hundred meters.

The two officers took off at a gallop. One of them stopped at about three hundred meters from the starting point in order to give the competitors the signal to take off. The other officer stopped at the foot of the oak to judge the arrival of the winner.

The three competitors departed simultaneously, forming a group as they passed the first officer. But when they reached about forty or fifty meters from the winning post, things changed. At that point, Caroline leaned over the neck of her mare, gave out a strident cry, raised her crop but without touching her mare. The mare now seemed to fly, passed the two horsemen, and arrived first at the objective some seven or eight horse-lengths ahead. Caroline quickly stopped the horse on her hocks, made her execute a very correct volte, leaned over, placed her elbow on her right knee and laughed mockingly at her two competitors, who, like gentlemen, admitted their defeat and expressed not the slightest rancor. The supper was on them. The two officers, happy to have served as judges, went on their way.

This goes to show, says Vaux, that in equitation, as in all the arts and crafts, a skilled workman can do good work even if his tool is inferior. Thus a good horse, well trained, performs with excellence only when handled by a skilled rider, whether horseman or horsewomen, military or civilian. In other words, Baucher and Loyo,

Une amazone—probably Caroline Loyo. Painted by Alfred de Dreux.

each in their own way, were the true creators of a new horsemanship.

Later, in 1881, during a series of cavalry manoeuvres, conducted under the direction of General Marquis de Galliffet, Captain H. Choppin met Caroline Loyo who was living in the village of Bléré to which she had retired. Her retirement was far from the luxurious life she had led as the triumphant *ecuyère*. Personal sorrows, financial losses, many disillusionments had embittered her. One had difficulty recognizing in this sad and mournful woman, the pretty, graceful, energetic, and fashionable former *ecuyère*.

In a modest house in the village, Caroline Loyo lived surrounded by mementos of her triumphant past. On the wall hung the portrait painted by Alfred de Dreux. One could also see many engravings of Caroline seated on many of her horses. She also possessed the autographs of many famous horsemen, as well as those of her colleagues, la Belle Madame Lejars, Auriol, the clown, the director Louis Dejean and many others.

Jules Janin mentions an incident that happened to him one day. A heavyset man, red cheeks, large stomach, but with the long and strong legs of a horseman, "the kind of legs that are able to completely surround a horse," asked Janin whether he had seen Caroline Loyo:

'Sir, did you see her, last year, on the bay mare she trained?'
'Alas, no, I did not see her last year; last year I was in Florence admiring the masterpieces at the Pitti Palace.'
'Sir,' continued the heavyset gentleman, 'when Caroline rides a new horse, one does not go to Florence, one does not go to the Pitti Palace, one goes to the circus.'
And he turned his back on me.
Today, one can go to Florence or even farther, since the succession to Caroline and Baucher continues to be vacant...
Baucher and Caroline Loyo have no more been replaced in performing *haute école* than has Rachel (the great tragedienne) been replaced on the stage of the Theatre Français, or old Laurent Franconi been replaced on the track of the Hippodrome when he rode Norma.[43]

Le Baron de Vaux is one of the few men who expressed enthusiasm for Caroline Loyo. Le Baron d'Etreillis, while expressing reluctant admiration for Pauline Cuzent, Anna Fillis, and Elise Petzold, says not a word about Caroline Loyo. One wonders why.

PAULINE CUZENT

The name of Pauline Cuzent became and has remained a legend in the annals of the circus of the nineteenth century. She was born in 1815 and belonged to the well-known family Jolibois-Cuzent made especially famous by her brother Paul Cuzent, one of the greatest acrobats on horseback, and her youngest sister La Belle Madame Lejars, whose beauty and grace were equal to her talent as a performer of vaulting and equestrian acrobatics, as well as dancing on her horse's back.

---

43   *Ibid.*, 119.

Pauline's talent as *ecuyère* of *haute école* came to the fore only after her brother Paul and her two sisters Antoinette and Armantine had begun to make names for themselves. It was thanks to François Baucher, who had observed her interest in the circus, that she was pushed into actually performing in the circus. Because of a slight limp, Pauline had been unable to vault, dance, or perform acrobatics on horseback. Fortunately, her father, Louis Cuzent, had been a talented musician and had passed this talent on to all the members of his family. Thus, Pauline first became a musician at the Theatre Séraphin where she played the coronet. She also played this instrument at the Theatre du Palais-Royal.

But Pauline longed for the circus and whenever possible, she went to see her brother and sisters work or perform. It is then that François Baucher noticed her intense interest and offered to give her lessons in equitation.

She made her debut in 1835 at the Cirque Olympique and then at the Cirque des Champs-Elysées and was an immediate success. As Vaux states, while not as beautiful as her sister, Antoinette, it was impossible not to find her charming when she appeared on Buridan, one of Baucher's horses. On her horse, no one noticed her limp. She always maintained a very solid seat and appeared graceful. As soon as she entered the ring on her horse, according to Baron d'Etreillis, she immediately became the "femme du monde, the ideal type of the elegant amazone."[44]

Everything she did was executed with the greatest of ease, exhibiting an innate finesse and a fluidity which she imparted on to her horse. Indeed, the disciples and admirers of Baucher always said that Pauline Cuzent was the only one who could execute all the *haute école* movements in the true spirit of Baucher's method and in the true spirit of French Classical Equitation.

While graceful and skillful, Pauline dominated her horse like a man but without force or violence. She executed croupades and lançades with her stallion, Auriol. When she made him jump fences, she never moved giving the impression that she was glued to her saddle.

It is interesting to note that while Baucher was forced, for financial reasons, to appear in the circus, for "*deux sous*" as he frequently repeated with derision, he had imparted to Pauline, as he had to many other outstanding horsemen and horsewomen, his expertise as an outstanding teacher. Pauline made it clear to everyone

---

44 *Ibid.*, 119-120.

that she was the pupil of Professor Baucher of Paris. In fact, there were two Bauchers, the one riding in the circus and the serious and innovative teacher of equitation.

Her work at the canter, her piaffes, her passages were always executed with the greatest simplicity and brilliance. To execute many of these *haute école* movements in a ring that measures only thirteen meters, the rider must execute these movements in a very tight and restricting manner. Successful execution of movements depends upon the use of this approach and of making the horse always move forward. Pauline had learned this from Baucher and she had learned to use his methods effectively.

While many of the horses that Pauline had been given or bought from Baucher were thoroughbreds who, before they had come to Baucher, had been racers or jumpers, Baucher had trained them so that they were capable in the circus.

Pauline Cuzent, François Baucher's favorite pupil.

Despite the successes of the Cuzent/Lejars Company and the addition of Pauline, the Cirque Olympique was forced to close its doors. Lighting, (gas lighting had just been introduced), had been turned off when the company was unable to pay its bill.

Without an engagement, the Cuzent Company went to work with the Cirque Loisset in the Netherlands. That circus returned to France in 1836 for the May opening of the Cirque des Champs-Elysées, the summer annex of the Cirque Olympique. Paul Cuzent and Jean Lejars continued to execute their equestrian acrobatics, as well as furthering their hippodramas. It was later in June that La Belle Madame Lejars and Pauline made their appearance in the ring. Antoinette was once again the star of the show. "Antoinette," says Tristan Rémy "is in the first ranks of the romantic *ecuyères* of the period."[45]

In 1839 François Baucher, who had never heretofore performed in the circus, was engaged by Louis Dejean and made his debut, appearing on his famous horse, Partisan.

Baucher watched with an appreciative eye the carrousels of the nine *ecuyères* dressed in different military costumes. Among them were Antoinette Cuzent-Lejars, Caroline Loyo, Pauline Cuzent. Antoinette also featured with Caroline Loyo and two other *ecuyères* in the Quadrille of the Middle Ages.

---

45   Baron d'Etreillis, Écuyers et Cavalier, autrefois et aujourd'hui, Paris: L. Badouin, 1883, 132.

With such talent, the two circuses, the Cirque Olympique and the Cirque des Champs-Elysées became the nursery for the various branches of equestrian talent. Unfortunately problems arose between the Director Louis Dejean and Cuzent/Lejars, and the company soon left France for Central Europe. Dejean was annoyed by their departure and did his best to retain them. He even tried to sue them for breach of contract, hoping that this would keep them in France. But he changed his mind and even offered to pay the transportation for Pauline and her horses, which included the famous Buridan and the jumper, Auriol.

When the company arrived in Prague they were now known as the Cirque de Paris. They were loudly acclaimed by the press which said that never before had anyone seen *ecuyères* of such excellence, executing acrobatic movements that only men had accomplished until now. They especially praised Antoinette, saying that her dancing with her horse was astonishing.

But it was Pauline who received the greatest praise executing movements of *haute école* on Buridan whom Baucher had offered to her when she left France as a token of their friendship. Buridan executed all the movements, even the very difficult ones, with the greatest of ease and without the slightest resistance.

Bernard Gutt, editor of the Bohemian Press wrote of Pauline:

We will never forget the virtuosity and grace shown by Mlle. Pauline Cuzent. She has a first class horse, it is true, but a horse cannot dance by himself....She dominates her horse like a strong man, yet it is

Pauline Cuzent.

competence and charm that she successfully demonstrates. Even with her stallion, Auriol, with whom she executes the most complicated lançades and croupades, she is outstanding. When her horse jumps over fences, she appears as though soldered to her saddle...[46]

Indeed, with horses such as Buridan and Partisan trained by Baucher, and the jumper Auriol, Pauline could not go wrong. But even with well-trained and disciplined horses, a mediocre rider could not accomplish much. Pauline Cuzent, taught by Baucher, had become an outstanding horsewoman. But her own motivation and abilities certainly contributed to her successes.

It was Baucher who had taught Pauline to execute one and two tempi flying changes. It was Baucher who had taught Pauline to execute pirouettes, or to execute an excellent piaffe, first low on the ground, then higher and higher above the ground. And what a wonderful piaffe she was able to execute on either Buridan or Partisan. Then, there was the backward trot and the canter.

It was these movements, executed with great skill by Pauline

---

46   Ibid., 19.

and her horses that contributed to her triumphs. Wherever she and her horses went, both the press and the public were impressed and applauded.

But problems beset the Cirque de Paris when the director of the Bohemian State Theatre, on the verge of bankruptcy, declared that the Cirque de Paris could dance on the stage but without their horses. Unfortunately Antoinette and Armantine danced better with their horses than without them. The troop took the hint and left.

The Cirque de Paris then traveled to Vienna to perform at the circus at the Prater. The press and the spectators praised them as usual. While the company was praised as a whole, La Belle Madame Lejars was singled out. The *Journal Illustré du Theatre* said 28 April 1845: "Madame Lejars was captivating due to her grace, her charm, her daring, and her attractive figure."[47]

And yet, once again, it was really Pauline who received the greatest praise:

We have kept our judgement with respect to the inimitable Mlle. Pauline Cuzent for the last. Whether she is riding Buridan, Capitaine, Robert, or Auriol, she never changes, for on each of her horses she executes extraordinary movements. The worth of this *ecuyère*, who is the first among all, and this is generally and unquestionably admitted, is such that even her competitors, past and present, must bow to her.

The Cirque de Paris gave its last performance in Vienna 28 May 1845. Madame Lejars danced the "Cracovienne," Paul Cuzent performed "*Les Jeux Olympiques*" and Pauline Cuzent rode Buridan, executing, as usual, brilliantly, the difficult movements of *haute école*. In 1848 the Cuzent company went to Saint Petersburg but without Jean Lejars, for he died in 1848 in Vienna. The company was as popular in Saint Petersburg as they had been in Prague and Vienna. The Cirque de Paris was not only praised for the performances of its members, but was also successful financially, having amassed many valuable gifts at the court of Nicolas I. Pauline was so greatly admired executing *haute école* that she became the riding instructor of the many duchesses of the court and other great ladies who showered her with affection and valuable gifts.

The Cuzent company returned to France and performed at a benefit performance for the Dramatic Actors' Fund on 25 August 1850. Pauline also participated, although she was in an advanced stage of

---

47   Ibid., 21

pregnancy, for on 13 November 1850 Dr. Vincent Duval announced the birth of a boy: mother, Pauline Cuzent, father unknown. The boy was named Jules. Antoinette and Jules Montjauze were present at the child's baptism. They also became his godparents.

In 1851 a contract forced Pauline to return to Europe and join the Cuzent troop. She also went with them to Saint Petersburg, but ill health made her return to France. She died 20 April 1852. The death certificate indicates that her residence was Meulan, the place which her sister, Antoinette had chosen after leaving Saint Petersburg and her husband so precipitously. However, she died in Paris in the Avenue des Champs-Elysées.

Everything she possessed was sold. A catalogue appeared, listing all her rich and beautiful clothes of velvet and silk, especially the clothes she wore when presenting herself and her horses, her furs, all her jewellery consisting of gold, precious stones, pearls, and diamonds. But after this splendid enumeration of her possessions, these unexpected words appeared: "*Peu de linge*" (very little linen). "*Peu de linge*," repeats Rémy, "This said it all, and this vulgar material detail indicated a whole life of splendor and lies. These words were pitilessly snatched at Death."[48]

It is sad to see how a talented and energetic family could lose its family members one by one at such early ages. The first to go was Armantine, then her husband, then Jean Lejars, La Belle Madame Lejars' husband, then Pauline Cuzent, lastly Paul Cuzent who died in Saint Petersburg.

Critics seem to be uncertain as to what they died of. Some attribute the deaths of Jean Lejars and Paul Cuzent to Asian cholera, others to tuberculosis or pneumonia. Pauline Cuzent may have died of tuberculosis. But there had been several outbreaks of cholera epidemics and pandemics in Europe and other parts of the world around the 1840s, 1850s and 1860s. Cures for cholera or any other diseases such as tuberculosis were unavailable at the time. Furthermore, the life style of artists, especially performing in the circus and travelling to foreign towns and capitals, was harsh and unrelenting. The bright lights, the applause, was gratifying and pleasant to the ears, but then came the cold lodgings, the hasty meals, the lack of sleep.

It is interesting to note what le Baron d'Etreillis has to say about executing *haute école* in the circus. Since the main concern of circus equitation, says Etreillis, is to please the public.

---

48   *Ibid.*, 23.

it is obliged to dazzle before it executes perfectly; the more ignorant and the more indifferent is the public, the more necessary is it to seek the means of stupefying and titillating it.... Even such brilliant practitioners of *haute école* as Laurent Franconi and his son, Victor Franconi," continues Etreillis, "resorted to certain grotesque movements. And François Baucher, although he usually maintained an equitation that adhered to the principles of French Classical Equitation, needed the applause of the public. While he executed piaffe, the passage, and work at the gallop with brilliant elan, he also performed the grotesque backward gallop, a movement which merely denoted man's domination of the horse and the horse being reduced to a machine.[49]

Etreillis also mentions one of Baucher's methods which was to work the horse in a tight manner to compensate for the lack of space in the ring. This, says Etreillis, actually results in a lack of impulsion and thus a horse loses his initiative, his natural paces, and he becomes a sort of automaton. It should, however, be remembered that the horses of the *ecuyères* when ridden in the countryside seemed to have all the impulsion they needed.

Etreillis has little praise for almost all of the *ecuyères* who began practicing their talents in the circus during the 1840s, 1850s or 1860s (and he completely ignored Caroline Loyo.) In fact, he seems to deplore the idea that *haute école* was primarily practiced in the circus by *ecuyères*. He seems to have forgotten that the circus was one of the few places where *haute école* was actually practiced and, more importantly, preserved. Thanks to these *ecuyères*.

Nevertheless, Etreillis has praise for Pauline Cuzent and considers her one of the few *ecuyères* who, despite certain extravaganzas, performed in the tradition of French Classical Equitation. Considerable praise coming from Etreillis!

LA BELLE MADAME LEJARS AND THE CUZENT / LEJARS COMPANY

Le Baron de Vaux refers to La Belle Madame Lejars only briefly because she was not an *ecuyère de haute école* but an *ecuyère de panneau*. He refers to her only in the context of her sister, Pauline Cuzent who was, as we have seen, very much an *ecuyère de haute école* and whom he greatly admired.

---

49   D'Etreillis, *ibid.*, 126, 127, 128, 129,

There is not much separate and exclusive information about la Belle Madame Lejars as there is for many other *ecuyères*. Since she was an integral part of the troop Cuzent/Lejars, what is available, is included with information on Paul Cuzent, her sisters, Armantine and Pauline, her husband, Jean Lejars, as well as the various circuses in which they performed.

La Belle Madame Lejars, as she became known during her period of triumphs in the circus, belonged to the famous Jolibois-Cuzent family. Marie Antoinette Angelique Cuzent, as she was initially called, was born in 1820, the youngest of three girls. Her ancestors were ambulant actors named Fuant who changed their name to Jolibois, a considerably nicer French name. The Jolibois were not only actors but also jumpers, jugglers, rope dancers, animal trainers, musicians, and later, *écuyer*s.

Henri Louis Cuzent, who married a Jolibois, was a printer in Brest. He was also a musician, playing the flute and the violoncello. This talent he passed on to his son, Paul Cuzent, a distinguished oboist and a fairly well-known composer, who became an outstanding *écuyer* and the leader of the Cuzent/Lejars company.

He composed much of the music for himself and his company, as well as for François Baucher. As has already been noted, Henri Louis Cuzent's daughter, Pauline Cuzent, was also a musician and played the coronet at the Theatre d'Ombres de Séraphin. It seems that Antoinette, La Belle Madame Lejars, also played an instrument, the *ophicléide*.[50]

Antoinette Jolibois-Cuzent-Lejars became most famous as an *ecuyère de panneau* when, in 1834, at the age of fourteen, she began to do acrobatics on horseback, vault, and dance on her horse at the Cirque Olympique. She was already then "the first and the most romantic of all the *ecuyères* due to the veil of mystery that surrounded her. And the passage of time" says Tristan Rémy, "only thickens this mystery, which becomes more and more difficult to unravel."[51] While Armantine had preceded Antoinette executing equestrian acrobatics and vaulting, she never acquired the grace and beauty and the triumphs of Antoinette.

While graceful and agile, Antoinette Lejars executed exercises that only *écuyer*s had heretofore performed. But she presented these exercises with such tranquility and charm that it never occurred

---

50   A keyed brass musical instrument similar to the tuba. It is a conical-bore keyed instrument belonging to the bugle family and has a similar shape to the sudrophone.

51   Rémy, *ibid.*, 5.

Antoinette Cuzent - Lejars, La Belle Madame Lejars.

to anyone, not even to Antoinette herself, that she was, indeed, performing feats that could be dangerous.

It has often been asked how and when did the Jolibois women, as they were initially called, learned how to ride when the original family consisted of a grandfather who was an itinerant actor, a father who was a printer and musician, and a mother who was an actress. While the question has not really been answered, it is safe to say that the three Jolibois women, Antoinette, Armantine, and Pauline, did, indeed, become outstanding *ecuyères*.

It was Adolphe Franconi who had noticed the Cuzent/Lejars family performing with the Cirque Loisset, then with the company of Laurent Lalanne, and engaged them for the winter season of 1834 with the Cirque Olympique. And while acrobatics on horseback had become a popular entertainment, Adolphe Franconi, its director, had to acquiesce when the new proprietor, Louis Dejean, insisted that melodramas on horseback, that is, pantomimes and hippodramas, be included in the programme. Thus Paul Cuzent and Jean Lejars appeared in a number of spectacles, such as, "Thadeus, the Resuscitated One" (a loose adaptation of the "Wandering Jew"), "The Two Chinese," "The Battle of the Voltigeurs," including an extravaganza entitled "The Great Cavalry

Antoinette Cuzent-Lejars at the Cirque des Champs-Elysées, 1840.

Manoeuvres" which Adolphe Franconi commanded.

Despite the successes of the Cuzent/Lejars Company and the addition of Pauline Cuzent, the Cirque Olympique was forced to close its doors, fortunately only temporarily.

Without an engagement, the Cuzent/ Lejars Company joined the Cirque Loisset in the Netherlands, returning to France in 1836 to the Cirque des Champs-Elysées for its May opening.

Equestrian spectacles continued to abound. A popular act, "The Royal Post," (originally initiated by Andrew Ducrow) was performed with Paul Cuzent straddling two horses, and at times, even four horses, with several other horses passing singly under his legs as he quickly picked up their reins. An act entitled *"Zazezizozu"* with activated figures on horseback representing chess figures, cards, and dominos, was a spectacular performance with the whole company involved. According to Willson Disher, when performed at the Cirque Olympique in 1835, *"Zazezizozu,"* was a Chinese spectacle about three princes named Zizi, Zozo, and Zuzu who all loved the Princess Zaza.[52] It is not clear how they resolved the problem.

Virginie Kenebel, a talented and pretty newcomer, joined the company, and became the wife of Victor Franconi. She was outstanding when she danced with her horse the, *"Cachucha."*

---

52   Willson Disher, *Greatest Show on Earth, London:* G. Bell & Sons, 1937, 173.

Soon, Antoinette, who had meanwhile become La Belle Madame Lejars and Pauline Cuzent made their appearance. Once again, Antoinette became the star of the show. "Antoinette Cuzent, la Belle Madame Lejars, is in the first ranks of the romantic *ecuyères* of the period."[53]

It was at this particular point in time that James Pradier, one of the best-known sculptors of the period, decided to sculpt la Belle Madame Lejars, for he discovered in the face of this *ecuyère* not only beauty but an expression of great passion. Louis Dejean accepted the request with enthusiasm, for he envisaged a certain amount of prestige for both of his circuses by placing the equestrian statue at the front of the Cirque des Champs-Elysées.

The statue represents la Belle Madame Lejars as Thisby, attired in a Grecian tunic, a chlamys on her shoulder, one breast bared with one knee against the horse's neck, the other against its withers. In her hand, she holds a lance with which she will pierce herself to join her expiring lover, Pyramus.

In 1839, François Baucher was engaged by Louis Dejean to join the Cirque des Champs-Elysées on his famous horse, Partisan. With such talented *ecuyères* as Caroline Loyo, Antoinette Cuzent-Lejars, Pauline Cuzent, Virginie Kenebel, the Cirque Olympique and its summer annex the Cirque des Champs-Elysées became the nursery wherein young talent developed. The Directors of circuses throughout Europe soon began to vie with each other for this talent.

Unfortunately, difficulties began to develop between Dejean and the Cuzent/Lejars Company. Refusing to renew the contract, the company left for Central Europe. In Prague, the newly formed Cirque de Paris, received outstanding praise. The press, in its enthusiasm, exclaimed that it had never seen such outstanding *ecuyères*, for they had executed movements that only men had heretofore been able to accomplish. Antoinette, dancing with her horse, as usual, received exceptional praise.

But problems occurred between the host company, the Theater of the State of Bohemia, which was on the verge of bankruptcy, and the very popular guest company, the Cirque de Paris. Out of jealousy, the director of the Theater of the State of Bohemia, decided to impose certain conditions upon the Cirque de Paris. "Yes," said the director, "the *ecuyères* can dance but without their horses."[54] The members of the Cirque de Paris had no other choice but to accept these conditions.

---

53 Rémy, *ibid.*, 12.
54 *Ibid.*, 19.

Antoinette - La Belle Madame Lejars.
(Sculpture by James Pradier)

Unfortunately, Antoinette and Armantine, dancing without their horses were, as a critic said "like fish out of water."⁵⁵ Furthermore, the music, which had been composed by Paul Cuzent, displeased certain critics who said that it was too much like circus music.

The Cirque de Paris left for Vienna. The reception on the part of the Viennese was loud and heartwarming. The *Journal Illustré du Theatre de Vienne* of 28 April 1845 praised the Cirque de Paris. But it singled out la Belle Madame Lejars, saying: "Madame Lejars was captivating in her performance due to her attractive grace, her charm, her daring, and the beauty of her figure."⁵⁶ The exceptional praise that Pauline Cuzent received has already been noted in the section devoted to her.

The Cirque de Paris gave its last performance in Vienna 28 May 1845. Madame Lejars danced the "*Cracovienne,*" a Polish National dance, with her horse. Paul Cuzent performed "*Les Jeux Olympiques,*" and Pauline Cuzent rode Buridan with her usual charm and flair. Since the Cirque de Paris was so popular in Austria, the company decided to take up residence there.

Armantine and her second husband, Carl Berg (her first husband had died young) traveled and performed in central Europe. But there never was any mention of Armantine on any of the bills or programmes of the various circuses. It turned out that ill-health had made appearances impossible. Indeed, she died in Paris 18 September 1847 at her residence in the Faubourg du Temple. She was only thirty years old.

---

55   *Ibid.*, 19.
56   *Ibid.*, 21.

Another startling event occurred, namely, the sudden so-called "disappearance" of Jean Lejars from Vienna on 18 October 1848. It turned out that the "disappearance" was due to his death. 1849 has also been given as the date of his death. Antoinette, la Belle Madame Lejars, was only twenty-eight years old.

When the Cuzent Company went to Saint-Petersburg, Antoinette went with them. There, she met the actor, Jean-Baptiste Jules Monjauze who had made his debut at the age of fourteen at the Theatre Montmartre. Madame Lejars and Monjauze were soon married. Monjauze also had a pleasant tenor voice and took singing lessons to improve his talent. He was engaged by the Imperial Theatre of Russia for the years 1849 and 1850. Meanwhile, Madame Lejars, for some unknown reason, left Saint Petersburg and her new husband to return to France where she lived in Meulan along the banks of the Seine.

Although now, without la Belle Madame Lejars, the Cuzent company continued to be successful, especially with the haute bourgeoisie and the aristocracy in Saint Petersburg and received from them much praise and expensive gifts. In an article entitled "When the Kirov was a Circus—Nicholas I and the First Russian School," published in Le Cirque dans L'Univers, Dominique Jando points out that Paul Cuzent and his initial company the Cirque de Paris (which had been renamed the Cirque de la Direction des Theatres Impériaux), helped develop *haute école* and the Classical circus in Russia and trained many of the Russian *écuyers* and *ecuyères*. Cuzent's company actually became the First Russian National Circus, which opened its doors to the public on 29 January 1849.[57]

The company returned to France in 1850. On 25 August of that year, it gave a benefit performance for the Dramatic Actors' Insurance Fund, to assure retired or sick actors some kind of financial support. This benefit performance included Pauline Cuzent who, as already noted, was in an advanced stage of pregnancy.

The company returned to Russia but during the Crimean War (1854-56), like many other French citizens living in Russia, they returned to France. In 1855, at the Theatre Lyrique Paul Cuzent and Jules Monjauze presented a pantomime entitled "The Infernal Gallop from the Last Judgement." The music was composed by Paul Cuzent.

Paul Cuzent had hoped to be able to devote himself exclusively to musical composition. But, dissatisfied with the results, he returned to Russia in 1855. He died in Saint Petersburg 5 July 1856 (the Paris

---

57   Dominique Jando, *"When the Kirov was a Circus—Nicholas I and the First Russian School," Le Cirque dans l'Univers*, 4-6

death certificate indicates 26 September 1856).

The last of the Cuzent/Lejars Company was Antoinette Jolibois-Cuzent-Lejars-Monjauze. Armantine had died 18 September 1847 (she had also lost two husbands); Jean Lejars had died 18 October 1848, Pauline 20 April 1852, Paul Cuzent 5 July 1856. As was the case with Laurent and Henri Franconi, some of the members of the Cuzent family most likely also died of cholera, which had, once again, reached epidemic proportions in Europe.

La Belle Madame Lejars returned to the circus a few times but was unable to repeat her former triumphs. Life, especially circus life, was changing. As Rémy puts it "the age of the romantic *ecuyères* has passed, and the '*biches*' (young modern women) of the Empire, whether they were *ecuyères* or not, had replaced them in spirit, for the *haute-bourgeoisie* of the business world had now achieved total financial power under Napoleon III."[58]

Dejean, however, remembering the triumphs of La Belle Madame Lejars, placed a second statue of the famous equestrian bronze of Antoinette Lejars representing Thisby, sculpted by Pradier, (Antoinette's horse was named Thisby), at the fronton of the newly named Cirque Napoleon (which changed to Cirque National, then Cirque d'Hiver). The original statue embellished the peristyle of the Cirque de l'Impératrice (named after Empress Eugenie).

Meanwhile, Jules Monjauze had "disappeared." Antoinette, by now destitute, was obliged to take on minor jobs in the circus.

Le Baron de Vaux saw her giving dance lessons and playing minor roles in pantomimes at the Cirque d'Hiver and the Cirque d'Eté after the Franco-Prussian War of 1870. In 1893, at the age of seventy-three, she was forced to take on the job of usher in the very circuses where she had attained so many nights of triumph. She died a sad and lonely death in a hospital in 1895. When her death was announced by the Société des Artistes Dramatiques, very few remembered that she had been immortalized by Pradier.

When the Cirque d'Eté was demolished in 1899, Pradier's equestrian statue of La Belle Madame Lejars, kneeling on her thoroughbred, breast bared, ready to die as she watched the agonizing Pyramus in his death throes, was placed in a warehouse. In May 1903, the press announced that the statue would be erected once again on the Carre Marigny on a small patch of grass where the circus had once stood. Nothing came of this. However, the original sculpture was bought by Edmond Blanc who had it transported to his property near Saint Cloud. The second statue of La Belle Madame Lejars also found a

[58] Rémy *Ibid.*, 23-24.

Sculpture of La Belle madame Lejars and her horse Thisby on the facade of the Cirque d'Hiver.

resting place. "With an Olympic gesture it salutes the passersby from the facade of the Cirque d'Hiver in the Boulevard du Temple."[59]

There is a photograph of this sculpture gracing the facade of the building which houses the Cirque d'Hiver in Adrian's book *Histoire illustrée des cirques parisiens d'hier et d'aujourd'hui*.

---

59 Ibid., 24.

CHAPTER VI:
MADAME MARIE ISABELLE
AND
THE ECOLE de CAVALERIE OF SAUMUR

As indicated earlier, Mme. Marie Isabelle is being presented in the category of *ecuyères* not because she practiced *haute école* or equestrian acrobatics in the circus or anywhere else, but because firstly, le Baron de Vaux placed her at the beginning of his long list of *ecuyères*, secondly, because he refers to her as an *ecuyère*, albeit with reservations. Strangely enough, he devotes fifty-one pages to her, considerably more pages than he devoted to more authentic *ecuyères*. She is being included for another reason. Her life, her activities in the field of equitation, her very presence at the École de Cavalerie, does cause a certain amount of amusement, if not hilarity. What is even more remarkable is the ire that her engagement to teach horsemanship to officers and non-commissioned officers at the École de Cavalerie of Saumur and to train their horses, aroused among many horsemen, especially on the part of le Comte d'Aure. According to Vaux there is reason to believe that Mme. Isabelle was hired, not only because she had a patron high up in the military or at the imperial court, but because those who had been and were still hostile to the teachings and methods of François Baucher, found that engaging Mme. Isabelle was a way of continuing to put Baucher in his place.

I am placing her in a separate chapter, not because she is unique but merely because she is unprecedented. I also wanted to discuss Mme. Isabelle's training sessions at the École de Cavalerie, the reaction of its members, the reaction of the Commission, and the end of this "mysterious farce," as Vaux repeatedly called the affair.

The following are the opening lines in Vaux's chapter dealing with Mme. Marie Isabelle:

The fame of Mme. Isabelle as an *ecuyère* of *haute école* is merely due to the fact that she was sent to the École de Cavalerie, for she had nothing else to leave to posterity. She was of medium height, with a short torso, her figure was poor, her bosom was that of a wet nurse; she also had a very ugly snub nose. In short, she was ugly. Married to an employee working in the Ministry of War, she had begun as a milliner. But when it comes to equestrian art, she simply does not exist and would never have existed, had she not had as her protector, a prince in the Imperial family.[60]

While equestrian training began relatively early in the lives of the other *ecuyères* discussed, with Marie Isabelle they began rather late. She began taking riding lessons from le Comte Lancôsmes-Brèves at the *manège* in the Rue Duphot, having suddenly become infatuated with equestrian activities, "an unfortunate passion" as Vaux puts it. She left Lancôsmes-Brèves because he insisted that she get on a horse. She then went to Jules-Charles Pellier who directed the *Manège* du Faubourg Saint Martin. Like the Franconi family, Pellier belonged to a long line of professional *écuyers*. What she found pleasant at this *manège* was that she was able to work in hand, which consisted of working with a long whip to arrive at the rassembler, the piaffe, the Spanish walk, pirouettes, and other *haute école* movements. Above all, she was enthused by the introduction of flexions, that is, making the horse supple at the jaw, poll, neck, and eventually collecting him, thus extending suppleness to all parts of the body, and, ultimately achieving lightness. This was, of course, the Baucher method. Since she was not forced to get on a horse, she was happy.

Pellier was a kind, patient, and conscientious teacher and gave her lessons every morning. But poor Marie Isabelle was "awkward," "unlovely," "ungraceful," "easily frightened," to use some of the epithets used by Vaux. Above all, grumbles Vaux, she was arrogant. "One could see her dressed from the waist up in the *amazone* attire and from the waist down wearing men's trousers after having removed her skirt. Her pockets were filled with pieces of carrots with which she hoped to wheedle the horses. Lumps of sugar and carrots were the basis of her method."[61]

At her disposal was a large obedient Dutch mare named Ravinette who possessed movements that were still energetic and cadenced. Unfortunately, when Monsieur Pellier's son took over the lessons when his father was indisposed, he caused much discomfort to Mme. Isabelle, for he liked to tease the awkward woman. Once she was in the saddle, by means of the crop, Pellier's son touched Ravinette, causing her to defend herself and making Marie Isabelle scream.

---

60   Baron de Vaux, *Écuyers et Ecuyères*. 55.
61   *Ibid.*, 56.

Eventually, Marie Isabelle succeeded in making Ravinette execute some sort of piaffe, the Spanish walk, and canter on two tracks. She even managed to make her horse execute lead changes.

But before her great day as instructor at the Ecole de Cavalerie came about, Mme. Isabelle practiced her method with the famous surcingle for a while in France. She then went to Austria and Russia to demonstrate this novelty highly recommended by Prince Jérôme, son of Emperor Napoleon III, also known as "Plon-Plon." She returned to France, determined to have her method adopted by the Army. She succeeded with the instructors of the Regiment des Guides and the school for staff officers. When her bout at the Ecole de Cavalerie failed, she went to England where she continued to praise both herself and her method. Her book, with its famous method, *Dressage par le surfaix-cavalier des chevaux de cavalerie, d'attelage et de course en six et douze leçons* appeared in 1858. She then disappeared.

But to return to her affair with the Ecole de Cavalerie, the great day arrived when she went to Saumur as instructor. This occurred at then end of 1854 at a time when le Comte d'Aure was *Écuyer en Chef* of the *manège*, when General Comte de Rochefort was commandant of the Ecole de Cavalerie, and when other excellent officers were in charge of the training of riders and horses. Everyone wondered who this lady was, where she came from, and where she had practiced her equestrian talents. How she had managed this, was a puzzle to many. High patronage, undoubtedly, some said. No one could believe that the Minister of War, a serious man, could do such a shameful thing as to inflict a woman upon the officers and non-commissioned officers, especially when the school could vaunt a number of excellent teachers, past and present. The younger officers were amused and said that if she is pretty and wears the tricorne hat well, then it will be fun. When she published her book on her method and the use of the surcingle and crop/spur combination, she indicated that it had been approved by His Excellency the Minister of War, and other important people, to be used by all the training schools of the French army. The work and her method, she claimed, had also been approved by his Majesty the Czar Nicolas of Russia, the Emperor Napoleon III, even the Queen of England.

Mme. Isabelle arrived at the Ecole de Cavalarie 11 November 1854. She was to begin her instruction on 13 November with the officers and non-commissioned officers in attendance. Strangely, Commandant de Rochefort absented himself because of some mission in Paris. Colonel Schmit, second in command, the squadron chiefs, the *écuyer*s, all the officers and non-commissioned officers were present in the *Manège* des *Écuyer*s awaiting the distribution of their horses. Mme. Isabelle arrived in a rented carriage. She was dressed in a black *amazone* attire, chapeau *haut-de-forme*, with a veil. The carriage stopped at the door of the *manège*.

And she descended. She was neither moved nor intimidated; she wore a smile on her lips. She greeted Colonel Schmit and Vaux. Vaux's description of Mme. Isabelle is not very flattering to say the least. She was presented to the officers who were not hostile but, rather, behaved in compliance with what was expected of them. Mme. Isabelle was very pleasant with one and all, especially with Vaux who was to head the Commission set up to follow the work of Mme. Isabelle, which also included le Comte de Montigny, a civilian *écuyer*. Meanwhile the horses were allocated to their respective pupil/officers.

Much of her method consisted of suppling the horse at the junction of head and neck (the poll) so that the horse could acquire a good position. This was to be achieved by means of a surcingle and a crop/spur dangling on one side of it.

The horse must be at least five years old when one begins his training. Using a snaffle bridle at first, he must be ridden along the roads and highways and walked for two hours a day.[62] Should the horse be of a fearful nature, an older, quiet horse should accompany him. With respect to this recommendation, as Vaux points out, this is not a method but a very general rule which many people practice. Furthermore, adds Vaux, if the young horse is already mounted and ridden along roads and highways, he has certainly become familiar with a rider and has been partially gentled. But, Vaux goes on, if he is ridden by an inexperienced rider, certain bad habits and certain risks could develop, especially when ridden along roads and highways without experienced supervision.

However, to return to Mme. Isabelle's method:

If the horse is ridden during his training sessions, he should be ridden again after these sessions for a quarter of an hour for the first six lessons, and, half an hour during the last six lessons. If the horse has been trained before he is ridden, the trainer should repeat all these training lessons by means of the surcingle. A horse can become somewhat excited during the period when he is being trained, to avoid this he should be walked three hours a day with a snaffle bridle. For the first session one places on the horse a saddle, the surcingle,

---

62   It is my understanding that when the horse was ridden along roads and highways, a snaffle bridle was recommended, whereas during training sessions a double bridle with a curb bit was to be used.—Author's note.

and a double bridle whose four reins will be attached to the surcingle at the first holes. The horse will be exercised at a walk, with a deconstructed equilibrium, forwards and backwards, on a straight line, for twenty minutes. (The term *d'équilibre decompose* [deconstructed equilibrium], used by Mme. Isabelle, even the Commission was unable to understand.) As one proceeds, the reins will become gradually more taut. First the horse will go at the walk, then at the trot. One leads the horse, accompanied by another mature horse, for a walk twice a day for one hour.

In the final analysis, Mme. Isabelle's method is primarily the use of reins by means of the surcingle whose aim is an elevated *ramener*, and to subject the horse to an exercise, at a walk, at a deconstructed equilibrium, forwards and backwards. At this point Vaux interjects that the horse, placed in a position that is maintained by means of the surcingle, is in an artificial position which could only be detrimental to him.

In summary, says Vaux, the totality of this method proposed by Mme. Isabelle, scarcely justifies "the adoption of her method by the Minister of War, whose approval was based on the judgement given by the Regiment des Guides."[63]

According to Vaux, the question of the surcingle is not that its use is in itself a bad thing; rather it is Mme. Isabelle's intent to make a universal panacea out of it and her insistence that its use will bring about wondrous results and eliminate all possible future difficulties. Which is nonsense, says Vaux.

One of Vaux's criticisms is the use, or abuse, of the double bridle during training sessions. Its abuse, says Vaux, lies in the use of force on the part of the rider's legs and hands with respect to young, unbalanced, and untrained horses, made to execute exercises before their hocks have been suppled.

Another criticism levelled against Mme. Isabelle's method is her criticism of Baucher. In the first place, much of her in-hand suppling method, especially the suppling of the jaw, had been taken from Baucher's *Nouvelle Méthode*. Nonetheless, Mme. Isabelle criticized Baucher for certain contradictions. "One must remember," says Vaux, "that Baucher was an innovator of a unique and peerless fecundity. His discoveries did not appear at one single outflow of the brain, but were, rather, the continuous and unending thoughts of the illustrious *écuyer*, and his attempts to continually perfect his work."[64] In addition,

---

63   Vaux, 76.
64   *Ibid.*, 73.

says Vaux, Mme. Isabelle accuses Baucher of saying that "the horse champing (*mâcher*) at the bit will indicate his complete submission." To champ at the bit, criticizes Mme. Isabelle, may also indicate anger and resistance on the part of the horse. True. However, according to Vaux, when Baucher uses the term "*mâcher*" he means the "relaxation of the lower jaw."[65] One can find this meaning in his writings in over twenty passages. Above all, says Vaux, when Mme. Isabelle discusses the relaxation of the horse's jaw, she is obviously adopting this idea from Baucher without giving him any credit. It is not her own idea. Having taken lessons from Pellier, who was familiar with and made use of Baucher's method, she undoubtedly got this concept from him.

The notion of making the horse, at a walk, go through a 'deconstructed equilibrium' is, according to Vaux, neither logical nor useful. It serves little, when at the walk, to make a horse stop in his stride, ever so briefly, when the points of contact with the ground are not simultaneous. While this attempt to stop the horse's stride has little value to the horse's gait, it can actually hamper a horse's free impulsion, especially when it comes to the walk.

When it is a question of the one-sided spur/crop combination, this has a tendency to disturb the horse's equilibrium in that there is no accord with respect to his impulsive strength. It is, after all, one-sided.

Furthermore, the famous surcingle which Mme. Isabelle so loudly praises will have a negative effect in that its rigidity will make the horse heavy on the bit.

The members of the Commission actually found nothing new in Mme. Isabelle's method. They (as did Vaux) found "the use of the surcingle to rein the horse, the 'deconstructed equilibrium' at the walk, the crop/spur combination, her work in hand,...to be of little significance."[66]

However, the first report, completed after the fifth lesson, was quite polite and encouraging, stating that "the results obtained with the double aim of making the, as yet, unmounted horse attentive and docile, supple and balanced, cadencing his gait at the walk, seemed simple and methodical, executed easily and without constraining the horse."[67]

---

65   Ibid., 74.
66   Ibid., 82.
67   Ibid., 82.

The second report, prepared after the eleventh session, repeated more or less the same ideas. It did, however, state that the crop/spur combination had little or no effect on the horse and that the riders had to make use of leg aids.

The third report, completed after the sixteenth session, stated that the work on two tracks, at the walk and the slow trot were executed calmly, but that work at the canter on the part of horses with only limited instruction, left much to be desired. That is, as long as the horses were worked at the walk and the slow trot, their movements were more or less satisfactory. But when the horses were worked on two tracks and at the canter, difficulties began to appear, indicating certain flaws in the method and that the progress envisioned by Mme. Isabelle became questionable.

In this session the horses were put to work by two and four riders, then by a troop, at the canter, without having actually been trained either at the walk or at the trot, which is contrary to all the logical principles of equitation. Furthermore, this is not the first time that [the Commission] notices this lack of progression with respect to the new method; today's results at the canter point out, with great urgency, the flaws in this system of training; thus the Commission finds it necessary to record this observation in its proceedings.[68]

In its fourth report, prepared after the twentieth session, the Commission insisted in its earlier statement:

"If one were to ask the Commission wherein lies the difference between work at the walk and trot and work at the canter, [the Commission] would not hesitate to answer that, in its opinion, this difference must be attributed to the fact that the method had not sufficiently prepared the horses to execute movements at the active gaits, and above all, at the departures and halts...."[69]

These criticisms which were not only accurate but also moderate, did not appeal to Mme. Isabelle. Undoubtedly, she must have felt the equestrian insufficiency of her method. To save face, she declared "that the instruction given to the staff officers had been completed and that she considered these gentlemen as having been sufficiently initiated into the principles of her method, and able to teach it after she had

---

68   Ibid., 83.
69   Ibid., 84.

placed into their hands her written lessons."[70]

The higher-ups then decided that the teaching officers and the non-commissioned officers of the cadre and artillery would receive her instruction.

Thus the "farce," this "huge equestrian mystification," as Vaux calls this whole affair, continued.

After five sessions involving the new category of riders, the Commission, in its fifth report, stated that it must formulate the same earlier observations. "The work at the walk and trot are executed with more or less regularity, but at the canter the same defect arises, that is, the lack of calm and all-out efficiency. This indicates that more than four horses have made very little progress."[71] Nonetheless, Mme. Isabelle declared that instruction in this category of officers had been sufficient, but that she would continue to round off the instruction with the non-commissioned officers before starting the education of stubborn and undisciplined horses.

"The further this comedy advanced, for it was a miserable comedy that Mme. Isabelle was playing, the more was she obliged to realize that her so-called method was a complete disaster."[72]

According to Vaux,

in the Regiment des Guides where, it is said, she has the protection of an all-powerful person, she had been able to throw dust into certain eyes and thus obtain a favorable verdict; but at the Ecole de Cavalerie she found herself in the presence of judges who were more serious, more competent, and she began to understand (for she was very intelligent) that things were different here and that the game she was playing could be and was already compromised.[73]

Vaux is certain that she was aware of the fact that her method was inadequate but that she refused to leave due to the large amount of money she was earning.

Vaux also believes that when she taught the captains and the officer/*écuyers*, men who were of a certain age and who were serious

---

70   Ibid., 84.
71   Ibid., 85.
72   Ibid., 85.
73   Ibid., 85.

about their duties, she found it easy to prolong those ridiculous sessions. But it was quite different when it came to the lieutenant/instructors, younger officers, less tolerant and more inclined to criticize and laugh at everything that sounded ridiculous to them. They were unable to take seriously "this *ecuyère* in skirts and even less, her childish method."[74] Thus it is understandable that after five sessions she wanted to get rid of them by declaring that their instruction had been completed. Whereas when it came to the non-commissioned officers she was able to cajole them and they were inclined to be more submissive.

Now Vaux comes to the third act of this comedy, namely the application of her method to stubborn and recalcitrant horses. "Now the mystification takes on greater proportions and the fiasco becomes complete."[75]

A new Commission was established and, unfortunately for him, says Vaux, he was asked to continue as its president with new members installed.

Twenty-two stubborn and undisciplined horses, taken from all categories, were put at her disposal. The best non-commissioned officers and the best under-instructors were to ride them. Mme. Isabelle had asked that she be free from the supervision of the Commission and work as she saw fit. Only non-commissioned officer de Novion was to be present to maintain order and assure that the authority of the instructor was heeded. Mme. Isabelle was to notify the Commission of the horses' readiness, which would then meet to examine the progress of these horses. After thirty-one lessons, each session lasting about one hour and a half, Mme. Isabelle wrote to the Colonel of the Ecole that the horses were ready and that she begged the Commission to apprise her of the movements they wanted to see the horses perform.

The Commission replied that a completely trained troop horse must be able to execute all the movements required and not only those movements for which the horses had been prepared.

This was accepted and on February 5th the stubborn and undisciplined horses were examined. Only seven out of the twenty-two horses seemed to have made some improvement. The others were still as stubborn and undisciplined as before.

The Commission was annoyed and stated briefly that it was dissatisfied with the results and with the effectiveness of the training

---

74 Ibid., 86.
75 Ibid., 87.

applied to these horses, that much time and effort had been given and that the riders and grooms had been distracted from their usual duties. The Commission was adamant and unanimous in its declaration that this work with stubborn horses be immediately abandoned. That the last phase of work should now take place, namely the training of young horses. A copy of this letter was sent to the Minister of War. However, the same influence that had made itself felt throughout this "comedy," once more made itself felt. On February 10th a communique was sent to the Commission saying that the Minister would not accept the conclusions of the Commission. In that seven of the twenty-two horses had made progress, that is, a third, it was considered that work with the remaining fifteen stubborn horses should continue. This work should include the horse Marengo, with the proviso that all precautions were to be taken so that nothing could happen to him.

With such a definite order, the Commission could only acquiesce. Mme. Isabelle, however, saw to it that the seven so-called trained horses also be included, believing that these horses had most likely returned to their previous bad habits. This was, indeed, what had happened.

The Commission sent another report to the Minister, "asking respectfully that the attempts of Mme. Isabelle be discontinued." It added that "because the mission set by this lady was a veritable embarrassment for the Ecole, her mission should be terminated. This is the wish of the entire Commission."[76] This time the Minister and his Ministry accepted the strong declaration with respect to the stubborn horses, but stated that work should be continued with respect to the young horses. "Mme. Isabelle, more arrogant than ever, continued to receive her five hundred francs per month and to parade within our *manèges*."[77]

Understandably, the Commission was not happy that its protestations were not heeded, but had to follow the wishes of the Ministry.

On 1 March work with the young horses began. They were ridden at the walk, trot, and canter in order to determine the degree of instruction they had already received. All demonstrated that they were basically docile, that they had already received some training, and that they were in good health. They were then placed into the hands of Mme. Isabelle.

---

76   *Ibid.*, 91.
77   *Ibid.*, 91.

On 16 April Mme. Isabelle declared that the instruction of these young horses had been completed. The Commission was ready to examine their progress. All the members of the Ecole de Cavalerie were present. So was a large part of the inhabitants of the town. A number of articles had appeared in the press, published by Mme. Isabelle, accusing the Commission of bias, and the angry reactions of members of the Ecole de Cavalerie, had aroused public opinion.

The event took place in the rectangle of the Ecole de Cavalerie near the large *manège*. The public galleries and boxes were filled with impatient spectators, curious of the outcome.

The result was disastrous for Mme. Isabelle who, despite her audaciousness and self-assurance, was thus obliged to recognize her total failure. The resulting proceedings, which covered eight pages, related in minute detail the event.

The outcome of the training of these young horses was deplorable, especially when one considered that these horses had received some earlier training and that the riders who rode them were the very best. The failure of Mme. Isabelle should be blamed neither on the men nor on the horses; rather blame should be given to the so-called method used, for Mme. Isabelle had no method at all. And what series of movements she offered were not new principles at all. This is what the Commission had been declaring all along. In fact, whenever a horse became undisciplined, she immediately put him on the lunge line, pushing the horse into a gallop with tremendous force by means of the lunge whip. The proceedings of the Commission repeated their strong reservations about allowing horses to go on long walks along roads and highways with little or no supervision; the surcingle, they said, was a German invention, a poor imitation of the wooden man, having all its inconveniences and no advantages; that using reins, attached to a surcingle, that were constantly taut, and with the use of a curb bit, could and would only damage the sensitivity of the horse's bars. For due to the surcingle, the bars become hard, that is, the horse acquires a hard mouth. Many of the officers who were part of the programme attested to the hardness of their horses' mouths, that they were heavy on the bit and on the hand.

The members of the Commission considered of little importance the use of the crop/spur combination, as little as did Mme. Isabelle herself, for she used it very seldom. It was only *ajoujou* (a plaything, a gimmick).

With respect to the deconstructed equilibrium, the Commission declared that it had never seen it being executed, that it did not understand Mme. Isabelle's explanations, and therefore had nothing to say about it, especially when it involved an unmounted horse. This training had now been going on for over five months and it was high time to end this grotesque and ridiculous comedy which, to the stupefaction of all, was being played at the Ecole for six months, compromising the dignity of the Ecole, and all for the "beautiful eyes of an intriguer, whose equestrian ignorance went beyond anything imaginable."[78]

The Ministry finally had to accept the Commission's verdict. Mme. Isabelle received the order to leave the Ecole. Once in Paris, she saw to it that articles appeared in the newspapers, more or less, injurious to the Commission, declaring its members once again, unjust and biased. And so ends the Mme. Isabelle affair.

Vaux then gives a detailed and interesting analysis of Marengo who had, some time before Mme. Isabelle's departure, been sent to the Ecole de Cavalerie, along with other stubborn and undisciplined horses, to be trained by Mme. Isabelle.

In order to supervise him personally, Marengo was placed close to where Mme. Isabelle was housed and treated by her with sugar lumps. On 17 April 1854 Mme. Isabelle stated in the *Moniteur de l'Armée* that she had trained Marengo "a magnificent courser whom the best *écuyer*s at the Ecole had tried unsuccessfully to train, even after having used all the science at their disposal."[79]

Added to this statement appeared also her famous method and the remarkable results she had achieved in Russia. Since the Minister had ordered the Commission to continue the training of Marengo by Mme. Isabelle, the Commission had been forced to comply.

Mme. Isabelle soon declared that Marengo was ready and that the Commission should examine him. Mme. Isabelle was invited to attend but refused to participate, stating that during the examination of the young horses she had been insulted by the members of the Commission. Vaux denied that this had occurred.

Since Lieutenant de Boisdenemetz had, according to the *Moniteur de l'Armée* "tamed" this terrible creature, he was asked to appear in order to ride Marengo in the presence of the Commission. The lieutenant begged off, saying that he had ridden Marengo under certain conditions, that is, after the horse had been subjected to certain pre-exercises in accordance with the instructions of Mme. Isabelle, that he had ridden him along the highway, accompanied by a groom and another horse. He felt that he could not ride Marengo alone in the rectangle.

---

78   Ibid., 96.

79   Ibid., 98.

General de Rochefort was asked to ride Marengo. He also refused. Then under-instructor Maréchale, an excellent rider, who had followed the sessions of Mme. Isabelle for five months, was then asked. He complied.

As soon as Maréchale mounted him, Marengo refused to go forward, began to bound and rear, exactly as he had done in the past. Attacked vigorously by the rider, he finally galloped forward, furious, clamping on to the bit with such force that the rider had great difficulty stopping him, a defense that he did not have earlier when he had a sensitive mouth, which he no longer had.

This behavior occurred three times with the same results, forcing the general to order the horse to be returned to the stable. This event happened in the presence of a large audience. Present were almost all the officers of the Ecole who had become indignant due to the falseness of the statements made by Mme. Isabelle in the *Moniteur*.

In the last paragraph of the proceedings, the Commission stated the following:

The Commission, while despising the outrages of a badly brought-up woman, for whom the lack of success had rendered furious, had, nonetheless, considered it beneath it to mention a particular incident in its earlier proceedings. However, attacked by a woman who had respect for nothing and whose effrontery went beyond anything seen heretofore, the Commission, out of a sense of duty, had until now remained silent with respect to the outrages committed in the course of its awkward mission; but it must now defend itself and repulse with indignation the wrongful accusations made by Mme. Isabelle.[80]

Vaux, using the words of the Commission, discusses the particular incident the Commission had withheld.

Marengo had been ridden by Boisdenemetz, but that a man, hired by Mme. Isabelle had walked in front of the horse, his pockets full of carrots cut in pieces and that as soon as the horse stopped and indicated that he was about to defend himself, he was grabbed and given carrots. In the course of a few weeks, Marengo became used to following this man. Mme. Isabelle then arrived in a carriage filled with carrots. Boisdenemetz got on Marengo whose glance followed the opened window of the carriage door from which Mme. Isabelle distributed her carrots. A groom followed on foot. But never had

---

80 *Ibid.*, 100.

Marengo been ridden in the *manège* or outdoors without being accompanied. And the one time when Boisdenemetz had attempted riding alone, he found himself separated from his mount.[81]

When Mme. Isabelle was given Marengo, he had not been ridden for over two years. Trained as a jumper, the horse, not mounted, was a marvel. As soon as one placed a man upon him, he became a fury. (It seems that he had been poorly castrated). After the failure of Mme. Isabelle and her subsequent departure, Marengo was given to under-instructor Chaverondier who, after several months of failure and being unseated innumerable times, became in September 1855 the complete master of Marengo, winning races and steeplechases with him. Thus Marengo, after the famous attempts of Mme. Isabelle, had now been transformed by Chaverondier into an outstanding, skillful, energetic, and courageous horse.

One important event among the many others that have been related here was the angry letter written by le Comte d'Aure and his resignation as a member of the Commission.

It is a rather long letter, discussing first the lamentable equestrian situation in France. For, says Aure, at a time when the arts, sciences, and industry have progressed, it is rather strange and discouraging that the equestrian art, an art so indispensable to every military and civilized nation, and which had reached its apogee in the eighteenth century, should be so neglected today.

Aure then mentions a few reasons for the decline of equitation, namely the abolishment of equestrian institutions, (the Ecole de Versailles had closed its doors in 1830), the turmoils of the various revolutions, and the disaffection on the part of the nobility and the wealthy with a military career.

Thus it is understandable that men who had not begun riding in their youth, and who, due to their present position, find riding necessary, these men, fearing to make mistakes, accept with great enthusiasm those who say to them "I arrive with a method which in twenty lessons, will eliminate forever difficult horses, regardless of their age and their temperament, a fact which no former practitioner has achieved."[82] Normally, says Aure, nobody listens seriously to these vaunts, but in our century strange things happen and there are people disposed to believe everything one tells them.

---

81 *Ibid.*, 101.
82 Aure, Comte Antoine Cartier d,' *de la Question équestre et de Madame Isabelle à l'Ecole de Cavalerie*, Pamphlet, 1855, 2

Aure then proceeds to remind the reader that the great success of Baucher, fifteen years ago, lay in such an erroneous promise. However, Aure goes on, Baucher was a talented artist, which is not the case with Madame Isabelle. Conditions have since quieted down, continues Aure, since the departure of Baucher from the Ecole de Cavalerie, and it was hoped that the Ecole de Cavalerie would be left alone to fulfill its tasks and not be bothered with so-called innovators. No such thing. And this time it is not even someone who is talented and who brings with him horses who are trained in accordance with his method and who can demonstrate a special kind of work. No, it is a woman who has neither method, nor talent, nor horses to exhibit. All she has is a type of reining gadget which, according to her, will bring about marvelous results.

Madame Isabelle apparently had addressed her request to the Emperor, Napoleon III, who then asked someone whom he believed competent to examine the matter. This task was given to the Captain/Instructor of the Regiment des Guides who then chose horses who were trained and used in the service. The results were understandably satisfactory.

Aure then discusses Marie Isabelle's method, a method that would replace all the precepts of a Pluvinel, a Nestier, an Abzac, a Bohan, and many others.

This method makes use of a reining device which, instead of using a snaffle bit as is usually done, uses a curb bit; instead of using a somewhat similar device known as an <u>*homme de bois*</u> (a wooden man), this new device is called a *surfaix-cavalier* (surcingle). Add to this the crop/spur combination, replace the legs of the rider and one now has to have three men per horse instead of the usual one. This is the method. With the surcingle, the crop/spur, and three men in attendance, according to Madame Isabelle any horse, regardless of age, conformation, strength, even weakness, can be successfully trained. This is her belief and that of the person who is her patron.

Aure then explains the use of a reining device: it is used to position the head and neck of a horse, which will give him the most appropriate and fitting position in his future behavior and make certain that when he moves he does so with regularity and elevation. Certain reining devices are always used with success in the training of young horses. But this must be done with the more gentle snaffle bit, which will not offend the horse's mouth.

A curb bit may also be used and has similar results, but here the result is more powerful, thus not to be applied with young horses. One can use the curb bit with success on older horses already trained, but even then its use is exceptional, namely on horses whose limbs are no longer set properly, who lean too much on the forehand, who are broken-gaited. It is a severe system, efficient and powerful, thus used sparingly, except in the circus where the horses are usually older and where it is necessary to regularize, enlarge, and extend the movements of the horse in a short time.

Aure describes the functions of the horses of the Regiment des Guides, namely, to scour Paris in all directions, and who, due to their work, have a tendency to become broken-gaited. It was thus quite understandable that giving them a break from their routine type of work and giving them regular exercise and the use of a reining device that rectified their position and movements, they could profit from it. This is well known and does not constitute a training method. However, the Captain/Instructor should have known better and not considered this method a marvelous panacea at solving all the problems of difficult horses.

The Minister of War should have ordered that the new method of Madame Isabelle be used simultaneously with the existing method, that is, two groups of horses of similar background should have been trained together during the same period of time, and only then should the results have been evaluated. Unfortunately those who pushed forward the new method did not want to hear of this.

Initially, Aure had been a member of the Commission, but as he states in his report, after four sessions had asked that he absent himself, aware that the Commission would be as bridled as were the horses. In his own report he testified that the reigning device used with the curb bit would be harmful to the young horses.

One would think, says Aure, that the criticisms and testimonies of the many competent horsemen would end the whole affair. On the contrary, Madame Isabelle received an even greater allowance and the promise of a large amount of money after her work at the Ecole de Cavalerie had been completed.

The order came that upon her arrival she be treated with all the courtesy and respect due to her rank and talent. Unfortunately, it was not to discuss her method or to try it out; rather, it was to be put into practice.

Aure quotes verbatim the introductory remarks made by Madame Isabelle: "I have come here to initiate you to my method by order of the Minister of War. I am not concerned with respect to the sanction or the criticism that may occur: this is a fait accompli, and you must subject yourself to it."[83] Those who made this decision, adds Aure, took upon themselves a severe responsibility, for "it is not a small thing to reverse, by a caprice or a whim, the equestrian instruction of a cavalry such as ours, satisfied with the means employed and to which it adheres because it finds them good and infallible, and which has the right to question the value of those that are imposed upon it."[84]

At the Ecole de Cavalerie, explains Aure, it was usual to initiate and to explain a system to the men in a rational and clear way. But this was not the case with Madame Isabelle, for she never gave explanations; neither did she accept observations. She merely gave orders with insolence and never accepted a reply, even when she imparted an equestrian principle that was an unacceptable heresy. Should someone say "but Madame, what you are saying is contrary to all equestrian rules, contrary to what is logical; she would answer "Quiet, it is my method."[85] This is the result of the exorbitant power given to her and the presence of a superior officer who is ordered to see that she is obeyed. However, if the officers obeyed Mme. Isabelle it is less out of discipline than out of curiosity to see how far the impudence of this women would go.

And this outrage, these turpitudes, says Aure, are happening in the nineteenth century to a nation that is intelligent and civilized. By whose authority does this woman act who has the impudence to say out loud that she will see to it that those who are submissive will be advanced, because, as she puts it, "she has the right, the means, the power of doing so, just as she will break those who resist her. The Emperor, the Minister of War must realize what is happening and launch an inquest."[86]

These lines were written by Aure in 1855 and published in the form of a pamphlet entitled *de la Question équestre et de Madame Isabelle à l'Ecole de Cavalerie.*

Aure also added a biographical note pertaining to the background of Madame Isabelle. A person, he says, who has occupied such public attention, certainly arouses one's interest and one wishes to know more about her background. What divine inspiration gave her this method, a method so greatly applauded by the press and so greatly admired and considered an equestrian revolution by certain persons.

---

83   Ibid.,4-5.
84   Ibid.,5.
85   Ibid.,5.
86   Ibid.,7.

She first entered a school of acting, le Theatre du Gymnase, but apparently had little success. She then turned to the equestrian art. Not only did she want to learn how to ride, but also to train horses. She took riding lessons first from Victor Franconi, then from Lancôsmes-Brèves, then Pellier. When she felt that she knew enough to be on her own, she went to Vienna. She was recommended to Prince Lisheinsten, who greeted her with politeness. She then went to Saint Petersburg where Prince Menschikoff awaited her and who, as Aure puts it, "already had his sights on her for ulterior motives."[87]

She asked to appear on horseback before the Czar of Russia at the Imperial circus. Unfortunately this presentation was unsuccessful, for the horse refused to enter the arena. Theodore Rancy, the principal *écuyer* of the Cirque Imperial, was obliged to take the horse by the bridle. Once in the *manège*, the poor horse could go neither forwards nor backwards. Rancy was forced to lead the horse out of the arena. The Czar gave Madame Isabelle a consolation prize, namely, a very expensive bracelet. As far as Prince Menschikoff was concerned, a far less gallant man, but more political, he thought it the right moment to send Madame Isabelle back to France to disorganize the French cavalry which he so rightly feared. Russia could not have had a more devoted and capable agent. (It should be noted that France was at war with Russia during the Crimean war of 1854-1856.)

How accurate is this last assumption on the part of Aure, is difficult to say. Throughout his life, Aure has always been a good raconteur and liked to joke. Yet, the presence of Madame Isabelle did, indeed, bring about the disruption, indignation, even shame, on the part of the members of the Ecole de Cavalerie.

---

87 Ibid.,7.

CHAPTER VII:
ANNA FILLIS, ELISE PETZOLD, EMILIE LOISSET, AND ELVIRA GUERRA

ANNA FILLIS

Anna Fillis was the daughter of the famous circus *écuyer* James Fillis who, as many maintain, was the equal of François Baucher and Laurent Franconi, in his horsemanship and in his ability to train horses. It seems that he superimposed certain distinguishing features upon the old *haute école* airs, making them more dramatic. He also wrote a book entitled *Principes de dressage et d'équitation.* Only relatively recently has his *Journal de Dressage* appeared.

James Fillis performed at the numerous circuses in Paris: the Cirque des Champs-Elysées, the Hippodrome de l'Alma, the Nouveau Cirque and in many of the capitals of Europe, usually on his famous horses, Germinal and Markir.

Anna Fillis was trained by her father and rode all the horses in the stable, well-trained ones and untrained ones. Her father stood in the center of the ring, lunge whip in hand, and she had to ride. To give her a secure seat he lunged her on her horse, making her stay in the saddle by means of her own equilibrium, allowing her neither the use of reins nor stirrups.

She made her debut at the Cirque des Champs-Elysées at the age of fifteen with her two *haute école* horses, MacGregor and Negro, whom her father had trained, as well as a good jumper. Of the many *ecuyères* who made it into the circus and performed successfully, Anna Fillis was one of the few to have made her entrance through the main door and had not been forced to start in the circus "nursery" as a pupil.

At the Cirque des Champs-Elysées, where she remained only briefly, she rode Gant, her favorite horse, Redouté, and Pretty-Boy; the latter was a beautiful sorrel. Much of the time she traveled with her mother and her three horses to perform in the capitals of Europe. They first went to Italy were Anna perfected her performances. Berlin and the Circus Renz came next where, with Gant, she executed the backwards canter which greatly appealed to the German public. She soon became the idol among all the knowledgeable amateurs and professionals in equitation.

To canter backwards was, for the amateur and dilettante, considered to be a great achievement on the part of an *écuyer* or *ecuyère*. Gant, a thoroughbred, whom James Fillis had also trained, was able to perform this movement with precision and ease. Anna also executed the canter to the left, in place, and the canter backwards; she then executed the canter to the right, in place, and backwards. The canter backwards is one of the more difficult of movements, especially for women. It is interesting to note that Fillis had trained horses to be ridden by women to execute the backwards canter with greater emphasis on the right leg so that they (and his daughter) could maintain that particular air with their single stirrup which is on the left. But, as we have seen, thanks to Anna Fillis' virtuosity, Gant was able to do the backwards canter on both leads.

With Gant, Anna was able to execute the more traditional *haute école* movements: brilliant flying changes at one and two tempi, the Spanish walk and trot, the piaffe and the passage. As a true daughter of James Fillis, it was the piaffe and the passage that were her forte. She was also successful in executing the passage in the form of a serpentine.

Everyone who observed Anna Fillis perform was immediately struck by her natural elegance, her charm, and her self-possessed and serene attitude. In all the movements she and her horse executed one could never see a movement that was excessive. This is why le Baron de Vaux considered her as being the foremost *ecuyère* of the period, one of the most elegant interpreters of French Classical Equitation. She was, according to Vaux and Etreillis, an individualist who, due to hard work and excellent training, had achieved such a degree of perfection that equitation was no longer a science but an art.

Indeed, Anna Fillis perfected equitation to such a degree that it was no wonder that she also became the idol of the Paris circus world. In her work one saw lightness and fluidity, effortless movements, as well as a harmony between horse and rider.

In *Questions Equestrcs,* General L'Hotte compares equestrian art with some of the other arts, pointing out that with the art of equitation special difficulties arise, in that one has to deal with two entities, two personalities, the horse and the rider. When one considers the dance, the dancer has only to contend with his or her own body, more specifically, legs and arms; with painting, the painter has to dominate his hands and the use of paint, the sculptor his hands and his special media. But a rider must take into consideration his own movements, his own body, his temperament, but also consider the horse's body and movements, his personality, his disposition, how he feels that day, physically and mentally. Without question, the artist, regardless of the field, must dominate his tools; but the rider has to communicate with his horse, dominate, but without force, another living creature. More importantly, when something happens to the horse, the rider has to acquire another one and start all over again with the long and time-consuming training.

The rider must execute his or her movements without the slightest visible effort, the aids must be invisible. This is precisely what distinguishes an outstanding rider/artiste from a merely competent one. And this is precisely the manner in which Anna Fillis and her horse executed their movements. Anna Fillis at all times gave the impression that her horse was on parole, that it was the horse who had decided what movement he was going to execute and how he was going to execute it, for Anna Fillis gave little or no indication that she was controlling the horse. And when one saw Gant execute his movements one realized what it meant when one said that a horse performs with lightness, fluidity, harmony, and cadence, when a horse's mass barely seems to move, when there is no resistance between the horse's mass and the rider's hands and legs.

Anna Fillis.

In *Un Officier de Cavalerie*, General L'Hotte defined lightness and fluidity in the following manner: "It is this very lightness that gives to savante equitation, to *haute* equitation, its cachet, its stamp of distinction, as well as to the rider who practices it the true distinguishing mark of his talent."[88]

---

88 Alexis-François L'Hotte, *Un Officier de cavalerie - Souvenirs*, Paris: Plon-Nourrit, 1906, 128.

Genral L'Hotte also makes an interesting comparison between circus riding and pure *haute école* riding. With respect to the former, it is the rider who is the active one, who makes it obvious to the spectator that all activity emanates from him or her; with the latter the rider acts passively, giving the impression that all activity emanates from the horse. Or, as L'Hotte sees it "the rider must forget himself and somehow become one with the horse."[89] This is how Anna Fillis performed: with understatement.

Anna Fillis had the same kind of affinity, that is, a special kind of rapport with her horse, Gant that other *ecuyères* had for one of their very special horses. And when such an affinity exists between horse and rider, it is truly amazing what a horse, even a horse with poor conformation, can do. It has often happened that a horse may be heavy, with poor conformation, or perhaps small, but when ridden by a certain rider, the horse can miraculously be transformed into a beautiful and astonishing creature, executing movements with excellence. This is what happened to L'Hotte when he rode his horse Laruns in Paris in 1866, giving him brilliance and lightness, so that when Napoleon III saw Laruns, he was so taken by him, that he wanted to own him. But when he saw Laruns standing in the Imperial stables, the Emperor was disappointed and returned the horse to Saumur.

A horse must have confidence in his rider, and Anna Fillis' horses had confidence in her and in her commands. Like Loyo or Cuzent, Anna Fillis never hesitated when she gave a command or executed a movement. It was this confidence, this trust, that Anna and the other *ecuyères* imparted to their horses so that they would follow them to no matter where, if they were asked to do so.

Anna Fillis, like many of the *ecuyères* discussed, also enjoyed riding in the countryside, where she was enterprising, daring, and loved speed; but in the *manège* or ring, she adhered to French Classical Equitation, exhibiting harmony and lightness.

It is interesting that it was an Englishman, James Fillis, who said that France could and should be proud of its heritage in equitation and for possessing such a large number of excellent *écuyer*s. And, one should add, an excellent number of *ecuyères*. For it was these very *ecuyères* who, in the circus and despite certain tours de force or extravaganzas so abhorred by some professionals and purists, especially those connected with the Ecole de Versailles, practiced and preserved *haute école*, that is, Classical riding, at a time when outdoor

---

89   Ibid., *Questions équestres*, Paris: Jean-Michel Place, 1991, 172.

riding had become so fashionable.

"Ah," said an old-timer, "those were women! Let us admit that they left us a name in the world of equitation, and sometimes, even in the... *demi-monde*."[90]

ELISE PETZOLD

During the 1880s "three charming *ecuyères* of *haute école*," writes le Baron de Vaux, "each in turn, shared the favor of the public."[91] All three were talented, all three were charming, each one in her own way, each one had differing personalities when they appeared before the public on their horses. These three *ecuyères* were Anna Fillis, Elise Petzold, and Emilie Loisset. In fact, continues Vaux, "one could consider this period the era of *haute école* as practiced by these *ecuyères*..."[92] Each one had her special supporters, each one her opponents, even her fanatics, who would sometimes come to blows to champion the greatness of one or the other.

Elise Petzold was the granddaughter of a rich soap merchant of Toeplitz of Austrian origin. When she reached the age of seventeen, Elise, as a dutiful daughter, was supposed to be married to a man of comparable means and background. But she was determined not to comply with her parents' wishes. The family waited patiently for her to eventually quiet down and acquiesce. Then the family moved to Dresden.

It was in Dresden that Elise's future was made when the Cirque Loisset appeared.

At the time Adeline Loisset, an aunt of Emilie Loisset, was performing. It so happened that Adeline Loisset was a friend of Elise's mother and one evening Elise was taken to the circus to watch Adeline perform *haute école*. It was love at first sight on the part of Elise for the circus and *haute école*. "I want to be an *ecuyère*. I will be an *écuyere*"[93] said the infatuated girl to her parents after the performance. Totally taken by what she had observed at the circus and by the woman who had performed *haute école*, she kept hanging around the dressingroom of Adeline Loisset, in the stalls, in the loges, and wherever else she hoped to find contact with the circus and with horses. She went so far as to steal a crop from Adeline and with this crop in hand she went

---

90   Adrian, *Le Cirque commence à cheval*, 32.
91   Baron de Vaux, *Écuyers et Ecuyères*, 146.
92   *Ibid.*, 146.
93   *Ibid.*, 148.

about town striking various languishing poses.

Her parents had enough of these antics and placed her in a convent, the Ursulinen Kloster, for a year hoping that with the passage of time the girl would get over this infatuation of wanting to ride *haute école* in the circus rather than get married.

Fortunately for Elise she found in the convent a soul mate, Sister Eugenie, a French princess, an exile and a refugee, hidden behind the walls of the convent for disobeying parental wishes. Sister Eugenie became her friend and while she did not encourage her to run away, she never discouraged her. Sister Eugenie reasoned that the year would go by quickly and that if she still wanted to become an *ecuyère* the topic could be brought up once again. And so Elise did not run away and the year passed rapidly as Sister Eugenie had predicted.

Elise returned home to her parents with the same *idee fixe*, namely, that she wanted to be an *ecuyère* and that she wanted riding lessons in *haute école*. Her father had a change of heart and allowed his daughter to take riding lessons from the famous Gustav Steinbrecht of Dessau. After a year of training, Steinbrecht, amazed and with admiration, declared that he had nothing further to teach her. The father was at first not moved. But the statements made by eminent and well-known horsemen finally convinced him and weakened his resistance. He even went to Halberstadt to see his daughter perform at the Cirque Loisset where she had been engaged. At first she only performed in quadrilles.

She was then discovered by the Count Schmetow of the Halberstadt garrison, a colonel of the Ulhans, a daredevil horseman. He was as well known in Austria as another daredevil, the Count Schandor, who had crossed the Danube on horseback over ice drifts. The Count Schmetow, himself, had behind him many a prowess of his own: one day he bore a message to his general on horseback, making his horse, with him on his back, climb the thirty steps of the honor stairs in three bounds. He halted his horse right in the middle of the antichamber of the general, delivered the telegram, and went down the same way as he had bounded up.

This is a typical show of what is known as "panache." A photograph taken in the early thirties in Saumur, shows some officers of the Cadre Noir sitting and drinking wine at a large table out-of-doors. An officer on horseback is in the act of jumping effortlessly over this table. None of the officers sitting at the table seems to show any fear that the jumper might be unsuccessful. As a matter of fact, they are laughing. Indeed, among cavalry officers, equitation is an activity that develops "*panache*," which means the development of *sang-froid*, esprit de corps, and *elan*.

The Count Schmetow discovered Elise among all the other *ecuyères*. He knew Ernest Renz, director of the Circus Renz, and told him of his wonderful discovery. Renz engaged Elise giving her a rather large salary. The Director of the Cirque Loisset where she was performing in quadrilles, now realized what he was losing and, in turn, offered her all sorts of advantages. He was unsuccessful and Elise left. She traveled with the Circus Renz to Vienna, Berlin, Breslau, Hamburg, Dresden. Wherever she went, she was triumphant.

Six years after her return from the Ursulinen Kloster, Elise returned to Erfurt where everyone had by now heard of her triumphs. All of Erfurt went to her first performance. Even her spiritual director and confessor of the convent went to see her perform. Elise, wanting to be tactful, pretended not to notice him. But this priest was so enthusiastic, so ecstatic, that he cheered her loudly, clapping his hands, and shouting loud "bravos." At the end of her performance, Elise had to acknowledge this noisy admirer, giving him the typical *ecuyère* salute and a grateful smile.

Five minutes later, the good priest was in the stables. After greeting each other, the priest said to Elise: "I bet you that you haven't paid a visit to the good sisters. Ungrateful one! Because you are with the circus? But you don't have to mention it to them... First you will dine with me. My sister will be so happy to greet you. But tomorrow you must go to the convent."[94]

Eventually Elise came to perform in Paris. Several critics claimed that her performance was too cold and too severe. But Vaux could not see the merit of this criticism. "The only criticism I have of this *ecuyère* is that she makes too many concessions to the public and makes use of these Germanic tricks, these tours de forces, for example, having her horse go down on his knees."[95] Vaux wonders why she feels the need to make her horse do these tricks. For, according to Vaux, Elise's horses are perfect in all their movements, well-trained, and easy to handle. Elise, herself, rides easily and beautifully, executing the Classical *haute école* movements to perfection.

Indeed when Elise rode Cony, a somewhat smallish horse, she rode with elegance and lightness. Cony was powerful on his hindquarters, yet light, and naturally well-balanced. All his movements were performed without any appreciable effort. Flying changes in one and two tempi Cony could perform effortlessly, head fixed, body

---

94 *Ibid.*, 151.

95 *ibid.*, 147.

Elise Petzold on Lord Byron.
(Painting by Edmond Grosjean.)

immobile, at no time deviating even an inch from the straight line. Cony's finale was perfect: he changed leads in place, did a *semi-courbette*, and was so graceful, his cadence resembled the regularity and cadence of the batton used by the director of an orchestra.

Another horse Elise rode in Paris was Etoile-du-Nord, who was as good, if not better than Cony, but not as beautiful. And not as light or as supple. He executed his lançades (disciplined forward bounds or leaps) like no other horse. "Under his graceful mistress," says Vaux, "Etoile-du-Nord resolved this special movement, which is basically disorderly and violent, with such elan and precision that one could actually count the three tempi."[96]

Both Vaux and Etreillis are impressed by the fact that she used her spur sparingly, that for her it was nothing more than a corrective leg, and that when she did use it, it was with great lightness.

Her third horse, Lord Byron, was given to her by the Empress of Austria, whose friend and teacher Elise became. Lord Byron was the pride and joy of Elise. He was a hunter and jumper and with him she was able to jump over all types of obstacles. Edmond Grandjean

---

96 *Ibid.*, 152.

painted him mounted by Elise. He was, indeed, the most beautiful and courageous hunter. Regretfully, one day, after having performed his daily work, he collapsed as though struck by lightening. That was the end of Lord Byron.

Riding outdoors or in the *manège*, Elise could ride any horse with the greatest of ease. While in the *manège* or ring, she rode Classically or savant and with harmony; but out-of-doors, in the woods or forest, or in the countryside, she rode enterprisingly and daringly.

As we have seen earlier, le Baron d'Etreillis had little praise for many of the *ecuyères* practicing *haute école* in the circus and none at all for the *ecuyère de panneau*. The exception was Pauline Cuzent who, as he put it, left a lacuna when she disappeared from the circus. Fortunately, says Etreillis, Elise Petzold came along to fill the gap. At first, continues Etreillis, he was skeptical of everything that came from Germany, especially when it came to the circus and *haute école*. "We were quite apprehensive when we heard about the arrival of a German *ecuyère* whose praises were sounded loudly from mouth to mouth."[97] It was with this apprehension that le Baron d'Etreillis went to observe Elise Petzold. With respect to a definition of elegance, Etreillis quotes le Comte d'Orsay who says: "Examining someone minutely from head to toe, in order to consider someone elegant, one must not find a single pin that is *de trop*; he must also be able to walk, during the day, in the most populated quarter without any one turning his head to look at him."[98] What Orsay is apparently trying to say is that elegance is discretion, a certain finesse and delicacy of dress, of behavior; it is the *juste milieu*. According to Etreillis, this instinctive charm, this quiet elegance of dress and manner, Elise Petzhold possessed it. It was noticeable the moment she entered the *manège*. "She rides in a way that is her very own, supple, graceful, and correct; her *amazone* (attire) are masterpieces which she wears with an inimitable grace."[99]

Etreillis is quick to point out that there is a contradiction in his dislike for the mechanical type of German equitation, and his admiration for an *ecuyère* who is a native of this very country. "We can only answer to this seeming contradiction that Mile Elise Petzold is an individual who transcends nations and who belongs to no particular school of equitation. She is herself, and it is what she

---

97 Baron d'Etreillis, *Écuyers et Cavaliers*, Paris: L. Badouin, 1883, 141.
98 *Ibid.*, 141.
99 *Ibid.*, 142.

does best."[100]

Etreillis then discusses her talent which, after having studied it carefully, he believes has reached perfection. It is so perfect that one has difficulty seizing it during its execution. Whatever difficulties exist, the *ecuyère* and the horse resolve them with the greatest of ease and with such simplicity that one wonders why one had never attempted doing it oneself.

Etreillis had the same reservations Vaux had when he saw Elise's horse going down on his knees in such an undignified way. "Do you have any idea how disgraceful this is" he asks Elise but only muttering to himself. "One would think that you attach to this movement some importance."[101]

This question was, of course, rhetorical and Etreillis knew this. He knew only too well that the average spectator was primarily titillated by such tours de force, rather than by a perfect pirouette, a collected walk, or a flying change in one or two tempi.

Indeed, according to Etreillis, the better the *ecuyère* was in the execution of *haute école* movements, the sadder it was for many connoisseurs to see her resort to these grotesque tours de force.

The appearance of Elise Petzold in France was and will remain a great event for *haute école* equitation. Etreillis believed that there have been very few women who have achieved the same kind of excellence. Her social position was also excellent not only due to her talent and background, but also due to her respectability and the patronage she received from the Empress of Austria. She was also admired for her reserve and strength of character and her own self-respect. "She rides a horse in the circus, but she is not a circus *ecuyère*... Never has man, who has had access to these two great seductions, woman and the horse, ever witnessed a more adorable spectacle."[102]

Unfortunately for the circus and *haute école*, Elise Petzold left the circus for good when she married le Comte de la Blanchère. According to Thétard, Madame de la Blanchère was still living in the 1930s. She was in her eighties when he saw her.

EMILIE LOISSET

Not much has been written about the *ecuyères* of the

---

100   *Ibid.*, 142.

101   *Ibid.*, 143.

102   *Ibid.*, 147, 148.

nineteenth century (with the exception of le Baron de Vaux), despite the fact that many of these *ecuyères* were extremely talented and extremely popular not only with the general public, but even with knowledgeable horsemen.

It should be remembered that during the nineteenth century, that is, the years between 1840 and the last decade of that century, the *ecuyère* reigned supreme in the circus ring. Indeed, the *ecuyère de haute école* looked very elegant and very much the lady, in her *amazone collant.* A little more has been written about Emilie Loisset and her all too brief triumphs as an *ecuyère de haute école*. It is le Baron de Vaux who features her, among other *ecuyères*, in his book, *Écuyers et Ecuyères*. She is also mentioned and greatly admired by Hughes Le Roux, Josef von Halperson, and Willson Disher.

Yes, Emilie Loisset, born in 1856, was a child of the circus. Her mother came from a famous circus family. Her grandfather was a famous Dutch circus director and attached to the court of the king. Her uncle, François Loisset, was one of Europe's best known trainers of horses at liberty and was for a long time director of circuses in Belgium and Holland. Thus it is understandable that the children preferred to go by their mother's family name. Many talented *écuyers* and *ecuyères* flocked to the Loisset circus, as did the Cuzent/Lejars company on a number of occasions. It was François Loisset who had trained Emilie and her sister, Clotilde, in equestrian acrobatics and *haute école* equitation. And it was Adeline Loisset, Emilie's aunt, performing *haute école* in Dresden, who had brought about Elise Petzold's infatuation with and later triumphs in the circus. But when François Loisset died in 1878, the Cirque Loisset was abandoned and Emilie and Clotilde had to seek engagements elsewhere. By that time, both girls had already become excellent horsewomen.

According to Le Roux there were, at the time, different kinds of *ecuyères*, the first consisting of young relatives of directors who were placed very early on a trained horse. They were usually destined to be *ecuyères de panneau*. At first Emilie and Clotilde were channeled into becoming *ecuyères de panneau*. A fall from the horse on the part of Emilie, affecting her left knee, put an end to equestrian acrobatics. Thus Emilie became an *ecuyère de haute école*. Clotilde continued to be an *ecuyère de panneau*.

There were, of course, those who did not belong to circus families but learned to ride as children, usually belonging to families rich enough to afford such activities. These were talented horsewomen who had learned to ride at an early age and became so absorbed with this activity that they opted for the circus—the only

Emilie Loisset

way they could practice and demonstrate their talent. This was the case of Elise Petzold. Or when a father lost the family fortune and the daughter had to earn her living with the only talent at her disposal: horsemanship. This was the case of Jenny de Rhaden.

In a way, Emilie also belonged to that group of *ecuyères* described by Tristan Rémy as forming part of the "*ecuyères romantiques.*" Le Roux in *Les Jeux du Cirque et la Vie Foraine* says that he saw her for the first time twenty years ago when she first appeared in a pantomime disguised as Prince Charming with her sister Clotilde. This was before her triumphs in Paris and Vienna. And, Le Roux admits, that when he saw her he fell in love with her. He not only admired her great talent, but was touched especially by the sad expression in her face and her smile. The following is Le Roux' description of Emilie:

> Emilie was eighteen years of age at the time. She was the most graceful creature in the world. But an astonishing sadness was visible in her face and in her eyes.
>
> I knew later that no flattering successes could ever overcome this wariness of life, this romanesque taste for melancholy. It was this inclination for melancholy that had recently made her rent a villa just opposite the little cemetery of the Maisons-Laffitte.

It was undoubtedly this sadness in her face and eyes noticed by Le Roux that had perhaps also appealed to le Prince de Hatzfeld to whom she was engaged. And continues Le Roux,

> May I be forgiven to have first evoked the melancholy smile of

the one who is no more. But I owe this salute to Emilie Loisset, for it is thanks to her that I already experienced as a child the revelation of the troubling beauty of a woman on a horse, this plastic coupling of two curvilinears that are the most perfect in creation: the stallion, aggrandizing woman in all her majesty; woman on the creature she rides, posed audaciously like a wing.[103]

Another historian of the circus, Josef von Halperson, was likewise taken with Emilie's charm and natural nobility, and comments on the "expression of sadness in her face, especially in her eyes, those half-veiled, soft, questioning, blue eyes, and her lips expressing a sad half-smile."[104]

According to Willson Disher, Emilie was usually alone, always dignified, always kind, and always greatly admired and loved. "Every day at the same hour she came alone to the circus. But when she claimed the ring, it was hers….After every rehearsal and every performance, she walked home alone to her little flat in the Rue du Cirque."[105] The inscription on the handle of her riding crop Emilie Loisset explains very well: *"Princesse ne daigne, Reine ne puis, Loisset suis."*

A contemporary of Emilie Loisset, Arnold Mortier, who wrote for *Soirées parisiennes*, had this to say of Emilie:

I would advise no one to follow her, nor to try to break the ice during this short journey with any conversation whatsoever; …she has a bodyguard ready to make a mouthful of anyone too daring. Turc, a dog as large as a Newfoundland, white apart from a black spot over one eye, has terrible fangs; he comes to the circus every evening with his mistress, waits in her dressing room, escorts her home, and sleeps at the foot of her bed…[106]

For a while Emilie lived in Berlin, returning to Paris to perform at the Cirque d'Hiver with her horses Ben Azet, Mahomet, and Pour-Toujours. Mahomet, a fiery sorrel, was her favorite horse and they worked well together. This occurs, perhaps more frequently with horsewomen than with horsemen: that there sometimes exists a strong affinity, even great affection, between

---

103   Hughes Le Roux, *Les Jeux du Cirque et la vie foraine*, 120-121.
104   Josef von Halperson, *Das Buch vom Zirkus*, 152.
105   Willson Disher, *Greatest Show on Earth*, 297.
106   *Ibid.*, 297.

horse and rider. As one examines the lives of many of these *ecuyères* one notices that they often worked well with a particular horse. And yet, after having seen a photograph of Fredy Knie, Jr. in *Le Grand Livre du Cirque* with his Lipizzaner, Capet, and the fond look he gives his horse and the gentle eyes of his horse, I begin to wonder if I am not mistaken. Men can also have this affinity and tenderness for a special horse.

With Emilie, Mahomet had learned to regularize his natural gaits as well as his school gaits, he had learned to feel at ease in his equilibrium, especially when he received the necessary aids from an *ecuyère* with tact and skill to enable him to execute the artificial airs. Emilie had learned to use only that force that was necessary to sustain the horse's equilibrium and to make him execute the airs required in *haute école*. This way she never unnecessarily tired her horse when she wanted him to execute the high airs or one of the special extravaganzas so often deplored by Vaux and Etreillis.

Riding Mahomet, Emilie would suddenly appear in the center of the ring, her horse doing a high, spirited, yet disciplined, lançade. Then the two would execute the usual *haute école* movements, including the Spanish walk and trot, and jumping over a set of candelabra. Before horse and rider left the ring, Mahomet would execute a number of lançades, and exit with spirited paces.

In April 1882, the 13th to be exact, after an absence of three years from her beloved Paris, Emilie Loisset returned with her horses, getting ready to begin her engagement at the Cirque d'Eté. Waiting for her engagement to start, she kept her horses at the Cirque d'Hiver and spent the time rehearsing them and herself for the opening day of the Cirque d'Eté. On that day of rehearsal, she decided to ride Pour-Toujours, a jumper of Irish stock, given to her by someone who had admired her horsemanship. And although she had used the same principles with Pour-Toujours that she had so successfully used with Mahomet, she had never really succeeded with the jumper. In fact, she had already experienced some difficulty with him in the past as she attempted to make her horse jump over a table lined with glowing candelabras. As he jumped, Pour-Toujours hit the table with his forelegs. She fell and dislocated her shoulder. She should have rid herself of this horse, as Charles Franconi had frequently urged her to do, but she refused.

On that fateful day, Pour-Toujours refused to jump so Emilie gave him a vigorous smack on his flanks. Pour-Toujours became angry, turned around in order to exit at a fast gallop. Unfortunately, Charles Franconi, having become aware of the horse's stubborn behavior, had quickly closed the iron door which is backstage at the entrance of the stables. This stopped the horse abruptly. His hind legs slipped, he balanced for a second, then fell over, carrying Emilie with him and under him. Emilie was mortally hurt. For two days she agonized in terrible pain. The fork of her saddle had punctured her abdomen.

This was to have been the *ecuyère*'s last season. She was to have married le Prince de Hatzfeld and become the fairy tale princess, as had happened to her sister Clotilde who had meanwhile married le Prince Reuss, a Prussian officer.
Her body was transported to Maisons-Laffitte where her parents lived and buried in the little cemetery just opposite the villa. Le Tout-Paris followed the cortege. Perhaps, as Adrian says, the death of Emilie Loisset symbolized the downfall of the equestrian circus where the horse was king and the *ecuyère* was queen.

It is interesting to note that Vaux, who always preserved a rather unsentimental view of the *écuyers* or *ecuyères* he describes, deviates markedly from his usual stance with respect to Emilie's accident and death.

I am unable to evoke this name without being saddened when I reflect upon the terrible accident that put an end to the glorious but, alas, too short, career of Emilie Loisset.
She was an incomparable horsewoman, of great personal grace, possessing a well-known honesty which she preserved in the kind of world where virtue is not always the rule..."[107]

In a book entitled *La Petite Lambton* by Philippe Daryl, we are given a fictionalized version of the sad story of Emilie Loisset.

ELVIRA GUERRA

---

[107] There is an interesting note added to Willson Disher's work, p. 299, which deals with a possible mix-up with respect to the dog Turc. According to Arnold Mortier, a contemporary of Emilie Loisset, le Baron de Vaux took the story of Loisset's dog, Turc, and his sad plight, and added it on to the story of Comtesse Fanny Ghyga and the sad plight of her dog Turc. It is possible that both Emilie and Fanny had a large dog named Turc who served as bodyguard and that when their mistresses died, they mourned them and disappeared or died, which is not unusual for dogs to do.

Elvira Guerra dominated the equestrian scene in the 1880s with Anna Fillis, Elise Petzold, and Emilie Loisset. She came from a circus family of long tradition. She was the granddaughter of the indomitable and famous Alessandro Guerra, known as the "furioso."

Towards the end of her life, in a letter to Henry Thétard, she explains that at the age of six her father, Rodolfo Guerra, had put her in the saddle on a Corsican pony. A few years later an English instructor gave her the solidity she had on the horse by making her sit astride on an Irish cob that had very harsh movements. This instructor lunged her on the horse making her stay in the saddle by means of her own equilibrium, for he allowed her neither the use of reins nor the use of stirrups. "I am forever grateful to him," she concluded in this letter, "...for I acquired a seat which allowed me to get on the most difficult horses."[108] Indeed, Elvira Guerra could subdue the most dangerous rogues.

Like Caroline Loyo, she trained her own horses and, like Loyo, she accepted nothing but an obedient and disciplined horse. Vaux believes that such a close and prolonged relationship between horse and rider was beneficial neither to horse nor to rider, for each one acquired not only the qualities of the other, but also the defects. But many of the *ecuyères* who trained their own horses believed that training one's horses had, indeed, certain advantages, in that one became even more aware of their strengths and weaknesses, their disposition, overt or secret.

One was also closer to them and became more involved with them. Greater mutual trust and dependency were thereby developed.

Likewise, Elvira would not accept working for a director or a circus she considered unpleasant. If that happened she would leave, even without bothering to take her salary with her.

According to Vaux, Elvira's riding could be regarded as what is known in the world of literature and painting, as "art for art's sake," that is, she had a purist vision of her art with no ulterior motive, no commercialism, not even for her own personal advancement.

Whatever she did, she did with an unsparing will power and energy. She was audacious in the training of her horses as in the execution of movements. She was well aware of the dangers she faced, she knew what the difficulties were, and was ready to face, combat, and, eventually, vanquish them. In a sense she differed from her predecessor, Caroline Loyo, who was also aware of dangers and willing to face them, but Loyo had first reasoned them out. With Elvira

---

108   Henry Thétard, *La Merveilleuse Histoire du cirque*, Vol. II, 105.

instinct and passion were considerably more dominant.

While Vaux says of Elvira Guerra that "as an *ecuyère* of *haute école*, after Anna Fillis, she is the best,"[109] he has certain reservations, adding that "she would have been the best if she had been instilled a little more... with the French [Classical] School."[110] According to Vaux, she lacked that delicacy of touch, her hands were a little too rigid, and she had more strength than grace.

Elvira Guerra

Yet, despite these flaws, which only a connoisseur could detect, Vaux quickly adds that the execution of her movements could not be criticized and that her work on two tracks at the walk, trot, or canter was irreproachable in that they were executed with regularity, fluidity, and spirit.

Elvira's special horse was Croziani. The two got along well together and what imperfections each one had, these disappeared when they worked together. Both horse and rider had an imperious disposition. Vaux believes that Elvira took advantage of Croziani's generosity and that the more he gave the more she demanded.

According to Vaux, in the stall Croziani seemed "awkward," "ungainly," and "heavy." However, Vaux goes on, when ridden by Elvira he was quite another horse, for then he became an astounding creature: his lines became long and fluid and he took on a remarkable lightness. This change in a horse when seen standing in a stall and then, when ridden by an excellent rider, becomes an astounding creature is not unusual. As mentioned earlier, this happened to Laruns when ridden by L'Hotte.

---

109   Vaux, 162.

110   *Ibid.*, 162.

Of Elvira, Vaux says that she had an excellent seat as though "fused to the saddle"; but, he complains, she was "a bit stiff." Vaux then goes on to say that she played with her horse as though she were a "virtuoso playing an instrument." An artist playing an instrument like a virtuoso could never be "a bit stiff." Neither could a rider be "a bit stiff" if compared to a virtuoso playing an instrument.

When one puts together all the comments made by Vaux with respect to the performance of Elvira and Croziani one has the impression that he perhaps observed Elvira and Croziani performing together on different nights.

Then, too, Elvira's problem, according to Vaux, was that she never consulted the opinion of other *écuyer*s or *ecuyères* and Vaux reprimands her for being too sure of herself, for her sense of superiority, and her steadfast belief in her own abilities.

One wonders whom should she have consulted. Once an *ecuyère* has been trained and has acquired considerable experience, it is unlikely that she would go and consult others. She may observe other riders during their performances and even take note of the way they execute their movements; certainly not consult them. Elvira had, after all, throughout those long years of training and practice, acquired certain traits, certain ways of executing her movements and those of her horse. It is unlikely that she would change them.

Elvira also had a little white horse, Sylvan, an Irish cob, whom she rode incognito in a circus in the suburbs just to see how the public reacted. Veiled, she would advance on Sylvan who strode forward like a fighting cock. Her concern about the reaction of this public was moot. As Vaux tells us, "a thrill of pleasure and admiration always went through the audience when they saw her and Sylvan appear. What caused this reaction is difficult to define. And when Elvira and Sylvan began to waltz, delirium broke out in the hall."[111]

Elvira had another horse, Compéador, trained in *haute école*. It was her habit to enter the ring executing an exemplary passage, the kind of passage only a horse with an excellent bloodline could execute. But Compéador was also a jumper. With him Elvira could jump over a table upon which were placed the usual lighted candelabras. Compéador always sailed over these obstacles with the greatest of ease.

Also in Elvira Guerra's stable one could find Diamant Noir and Rubis, both elegant horses, light and supple. With Bouton d'Or, Elvira was successful at the Concours Hippique de Paris.

---

111   *Ibid.*, 166.

Elvira Guerra on Bouton d'Or.

Elvira also had another talent. In her free and quiet hours she painted acquarelles of animals and flowers. In company she was an excellent conversationalist, able to converse on many subjects.

Elvira also taught equitation. In her letter to Thétard which she wrote shortly before her death, she also spoke of her teaching young pupils the art of equitation.

I taught all my pupils the most Classical, savant and correct airs of *haute école* to satisfy the most demanding connoisseurs. But I also taught them the most extravagant tricks so that they could satisfy the public, for example, having the horse walk on his hind legs with the rider mounted, executing pirouettes highly arched, walking on his knees, waltzing first slowly, then faster and faster, finally at full speed, doing the highest lançades.[112]

It is obvious that Elvira loved her work with a passion, working more, as Vaux states, to please herself; but also, as this letter to Thétard seems to imply, perhaps not only performing for "art for art's sake," but executing some tours de force, as she herself admits,

---

112 Thétard, Vol. II, 197.

to titillate the public. Still, because she taught her pupils to execute certain tours de force simply to satisfy the public, does not mean that when she performed them it was merely to please her public. In general, she preferred to satisfy herself with her work. And while abhorred by Vaux and Etreillis, these tours de force may also have been executed to please herself, to satisfy her daring personality and perform con brio.

Critics such as Vaux often appear inconsistent when on the one hand they criticize an *ecuyère* for paying too much attention to the public and, on the other hand, reprimanding them for ignoring the public as supposedly Elvira Guerra did.

One also detects somewhere between the lines on the part of Vaux and Etreillis, a half-hearted praise for anyone who did not specifically go through the French Classical School of Equitation. Praise for Elise Petzold (whose trainer was Gustav Steinbrecht) was given by Vaux and Etreillis, yet, one senses, it was given somewhat reluctantly. Praise for Elvira Guerra, although she did not belong to the German School of equitation, was given by Vaux rather hesitantly. Perhaps the fact that France had been besieged by the Prussians during the Franco-Prussian war of 1870, followed by the bombardment of Paris in order to terrorize the inhabitants into surrender, may have contributed to the kind of enmity that seems to underline, albeit subtly, the statements made by Vaux and Etreillis with respect to *ecuyères* who had received training other than in the French Classical School.

CHAPTER VIII:
COMTESSE FANNY GHYGA AND LA BARONNE JENNY de RHADEN

COMTESSE FANNY GHYGA

Fanny Ghyga was of Hungarian origin, born on a large plantation where she spent much of her childhood. One could usually find her on horseback, which was her great passion, riding at breakneck speed. She then was obliged to do her parents' bidding and marry, as all girls of a certain milieu had to do, albeit reluctantly. She married one of the most distinguished officers of the Serbian Army.

No details are available, but we do know that soon after her marriage, she wanted her freedom. She asked for a divorce which her husband would not grant. She wanted her freedom so much that when a travelling circus set up an enclosure nearby and gave equestrian performances, she decided to leave her home and husband and travel with the members of the circus the following day. It has also been rumored that she fell in love with one of the artists of the circus.

We are not sure where and with whom she learned *haute école* equitation, but we soon find her executing *haute école* movements in Saint Petersburg, Moscow, and Vienna. It was in Vienna that Director Charles Zidler saw her performing and engaged her to perform at the Hippodrome in Paris.

She was, as Vaux states, very much an individualist, both in her lifestyle as in her riding. She always dressed in extravagant clothes when performing. "She always remained herself, she resembled no other *ecuyère*."[113] She was determined to succeed, and when on horseback "what she wanted, she succeeded in achieving it."[114]

While she did, indeed, execute *haute école* movements, Vaux does not spend much time describing her performance as an *ecuyère* of *haute école*. According to Vaux, much of her performance seems to have involved the typical extravagant tricks that Vaux deplores so much: picking up a veil or a handkerchief off the ground from the horse's back, jumping over a table on which sat lighted candelabras, making the horse kneel or rear, extravaganzas in which even the best *haute école ecuyères* indulged. As Vaux has continually pointed

---

113   Baron de Vaux, *Écuyers et Ecuyères*, 140.
114   *Ibid.*, 140.

out, this required more courage than art. In fact, says Vaux, the poor woman, that is, Fanny Ghyga, like so many other *ecuyères*, was the victim of an excessive temerity. She was too confident in her abilities and often when she presented herself and her horse to the public, she had the bad habit of devoting herself totally, smile and all, to the public in the second and third galleries and forgot to concern herself with the behavior of her horse and the actual movement and direction in which they were going.

She was especially the idol of the second and third galleries and was usually smiling at and posing for them. This happened on the very last day of her engagement in 1881. She was, according to Vaux, as usual posing and smiling and paying no attention to what her horse was doing.

Unfortunately, her horse, whose hocks, according to Vaux, were somewhat flawed, suddenly aware that he was not being controlled, stumbled. He quickly but very awkwardly regained his balance at the very moment when she was swaying her hips with affectation, as she usually did. Fanny, surprised by the horse's stumble and his abrupt attempt to regain his balance, was unseated. Unfortunately, she was unable to remove her foot from the stirrup iron. She was thus dragged around the large, oval arena of the Hippodrome, her head bloody, and unconscious. Her foot still in the stirrup, she regained consciousness, but could not put her leg on the ground. She was in terrible pain. She was taken to the Beaujon hospital. The chief surgeon, Docteur Lefort, arrived, examined her leg, and since he could not find a break, decided not the amputate it. Two days later, Fanny's leg was badly swollen, for gangrene had set in. Nothing could be done for her.

When she died, at the age of twenty-four, she still wore the clothes and jewels she had been wearing during her performance that fatal night in the circus. The night the accident happened, her dog, Turc, a mastiff, waited for her as usual.

Since she had neither parents nor an admirer to protect her, Turc served as her bodyguard. He always came with Fanny to the circus in the evening and waited for her to finish her performance and then escort her back to where she was living. He slept at her bedside.

Unfortunately, that fateful night after the accident nobody paid any attention to the poor dog. He was lying as usual in the stall, waiting for his mistress. He waited until the last of the *écuyers* had gone home. He waited in vain. He finally left for the pension where they lived. He returned the next day, ears down, emitting now and then a terrible howl. He was given some food, which he refused. They tried to keep him, but he refused any kind of friendly gesture. On the third day he no longer returned to the circus. Nobody knew where he was or what had happened to him. Perhaps as a typical nineteenth century romantic gesture, he died on the tomb of his mistress.

It is interesting to note that almost all the *ecuyères* lived or traveled with a member of the family who served as chaperon. Jenny de Rhaden had her father and her aunt, later her husband. Anna Fillis traveled with her mother. The three Jolibois-Cuzent sisters lived and traveled with brother, husbands, and, of course, each other. Since Fanny Ghyga had no human to serve as chaperon, she had the mastiff, Turc, to protect her.[115]

LA BARONNE JENNY de RHADEN

Jenny de Rhaden was one of the few *ecuyères* of the nineteenth century to write her autobiography. In the introduction to her memoirs she tells us that for two years she has been experiencing terrible uninterrupted torments. She is afflicted with physical pain but, more importantly, with emotional pain brought about by life's deceptions. She spends her days in solitude, experiencing an acute sense of powerlessness. She finds refuge in a corner of her humble room, yet its walls give her a sense of suffocation. She finds no solace during the nights for she suffers from insomnia and her phantoms become even larger. Only when dawn begins to break does she fall into a sort of drowsiness. But the noises from the street soon awaken her.

Jenny is blind. She has been unable to adapt herself to this affliction. Better would it have been to be deaf or mute. But blindness makes her helpless. She believes that a person blind from birth could have adapted herself better than someone who had become blind at the age of thirty. Only recently did one of the specialists attending her have the courage to reveal that her blindness was permanent. With no hope of recovery she fell into despair. She "had to renounce the pleasures of living."[116] She attempted to ignore "the Phantom of Resignation"[117] but in vain.

Where is that youth of hers spent in joy and ease? She asks herself. Gone. But a glimmer of hope returns. She still has her memory, memories of this lost youth, her travels, her triumphs as an *ecuyère*,

---

115 See note 107 of the section dealing with Emilie Loisset of Chapter VII and the supposed mix-up. Fanny Ghyga apparently also had a large dog named Turc who served as a bodyguard.

116 Jenny de Rhaden, *Autobiographie—Le Roman d'une Ecuyère*,

117 *Ibid*, 7.

beloved faces, and familiar silhouettes. "I shall now attempt to unravel the chaos and draw out the salient faces and episodes... and try to present everything in an orderly fashion."[118]

She then asks the understanding public to show a charitable interest in the brief autobiography of an unhappy soul, just as in the past this public had given her enthusiastic applause to the equestrian developments of the *ecuyère*.

Jenny was born Eugenie Weiss in Breslau, Germany in a "beautiful villa in the rue des Jardins"[119] on a stormy winter's night. The birth of the baby put her mother into a coma. Yet the baby's first cry awakened the mother from the coma, but after expressing a moment of joy at the sight of the child, she fell back and died. The storm and the death of her mother were auspicious signs to Jenny, which soon became a conviction that her life was marred.

While the family lived in comfort and ease, there were frequent setbacks. The father gambled at the bourse (stock exchange), often losing considerable sums of money. After the death of his wife (he had promised her that he would take good care of the child and never remarry), he sent for an older cousin from Brittany to take care of Jenny and the household. "Tantante" gave Jenny the love and attention she needed.

Jenny was a delicate child. Constantly surrounded by adults gave her a precocious gravity. She was also spoiled. At the age of five she was sent to the pensionnat [boarding school] of Mademoiselle X, a well-known institution for girls. Because of her alert expression and her self-assurance, she was also spoiled and indulged at school.

Since her father possessed superb horses and kept an elegant equipage, it is understandable that she would be attracted to horses. When she was older her only wish was to follow her father on his morning rides. On one of these rides, a colonel, known to them and who commanded a cavalry regiment, expressed admiration for the young girl's excellent posture, and how solidly she sat on the horse; this gave Jenny the desire to take serious lessons in equitation. After fifteen lessons she was able to participate in a competitive rally. At seventeen she left school and was to be presented to the fashionable world of Breslau. "It is at this moment that the hardest knock occurred to a girl used to the gentle life of ease and luxury, namely the complete loss of the family fortune."[120] Playing again at the bourse, the father lost all.

---

118   *Ibid.*, 8.

119   *Ibid.*, 9.

120   *Ibid.*, 16.

Returning from a ride, as she dismounted, her dress *à la amazone* got caught in the saddle and tore. She asked herself, is this one of those signs? She rushed to her father's study and found him laying on the sofa, immersed in blood, a bullet hole in his chest.
"My dear girl, I am ruined. I prefer to die than live in poverty. Forgive me." The doctor was called. "Don't die," Jenny cried out, melodramatically, "I'll take care of things."[121] He did not die.

How was Jenny to take care of things? Of course, it was hoped that a rich marriage would take care of the family's predicament. But Jenny refused to be "sold" into matrimony, as she expressed it.

At that time, the famous Circus Renz of Berlin was performing in Breslau. The belief that *ecuyères* performing *haute école* in the circus earned "money like crazy" and her own excellent riding, contributed to Jenny's desire to perform in the circus and earn money. But, she adds, "it is evident that I had an absolutely erroneous idea what the career of an *ecuyère* of *haute école* was like, which I eventually discovered and which led to my disillusionment."[122]

She took lessons from the well-known professor of equitation Gaike. After two months of intensive lessons Jenny believed she was ready, that is, that she was an accomplished artiste. With the remains of her mother's heritage she bought the three horses required by an *ecuyère*: a warmblood from the stud of Trakehnen, a pure blood Arabian, both for *haute école*, and a six year old stallion to serve as jumper. These three horses had been trained in *haute école* on the property of the illustrious *écuyer*, the Baron Maas.

Jenny wrote to all the well-known circuses in Europe. While answering politely, they claimed that they had no opening at the moment for a beginner. Eventually she received an offer from the director of the Circus Salamonsky who offered her 300 hundred gold rubles (fifteen hundred francs) per month. She accepted and, accompanied by her father and "Tantante," left for Riga where the circus was currently performing.

The first night in Riga had been a sleepless one filled with anxiety. Her misgivings increased when she saw the miserable wooden circus covered with a dirty sailcloth. The director and his wife gave her a cold reception. She was told to saddle her horse and ride. While riding, Salamonsky was reading his newspaper, his wife was exchanging remarks with one of the *écuyer*s. When Jenny later asked Madame Salamonsky whether she was satisfied, she was told "Tell me, my child,...

---

121 *Ibid.*, 17.

122 *Ibid.*, 19.

Jenny de Rhaden

you assume that you will be receiving three hundred rubles per month. But to get this money you must first and foremost learn how to ride."[123] Stunned at this reception, Jenny decided to return to Breslau. That same evening, on their way to the circus to fetch her horses, the director told her to give her first performance the following day. "But without any remuneration. You must first learn how to ride."[124] In all fairness to the director and his wife, it is possible that what the Salamonskys meant was that Jenny had not yet learned to ride in the idiom of the circus but was executing pure *haute école* movements and that she was not yet an artist..

Jenny stayed. When she performed the following day, the public loved her, signaling that perhaps she had greater talent than many other more experienced *ecuyères*. Before performing that first night, she had asked her father to give her a glass of wine to settle her fears which resulted in a sort of anesthesia. When she heard the applause, she came to, realizing that she had actually performed.

The director now realized that he had someone of potential talent but he continued to treat her as though she were inferior and still refused to pay her. Even worse, the director coveted her black stallion and offered to buy him. Since her purse was empty, she had no other choice. In exchange she was given a mare jumper.

The editor-in-chief of the influential *Gazette de Duna* published a series of articles praising Jenny's horsemanship. He went so far as to criticize the treatment she was receiving. This resulted in an acceptable salary but also the jealousy of the director's wife, also an *ecuyère*,

---

123   Ibid.,24.

124   Ibid., 25.

who feared being eclipsed by Jenny. So Jenny was sent off to Moscow where the circus had an affiliate. There the public also applauded her performance enthusiastically.

Despite the harsh treatment she had received at the Circus Salamonsky, Jenny still had a warm feeling for it, for it had contributed to her first triumph. From Moscow she went to the Cirque Ciniselli in Saint Petersburg. The Director, Andro Ciniselli, the former *écuyer* to the King of Italy, was a charming old man and life became quite pleasant. The public loved her. Unfortunately, she aroused the jealousy of his daughters-in-law, also *ecuyères*.

"In its naiveté, the public sees only the brilliant aspects of the profession of a great *ecuyère*. But there is also the other side of the coin. All professions have their darker sides, and this one more than others."[125] She is, of course, referring to the wives or daughters of circus directors who believe that they are outstanding artists of *haute école*. But when an *ecuyère* of *haute école* appears, one who trains her own horses, and, thanks to her performance, manages to eclipse them, they try to make life difficult for her.

It so happened that the Baron Oscar Vladimirovich von Rhaden arrived in Saint Petersburg and met Jenny. His father was the vice-governor of Estlandia, his mother, born Baroness von Kleist. He was destined to be a successful officer in the Russian navy, but constant duels with other officers, frequently over their wives, eternally in debt due to gambling, got him into trouble with his superiors. But family contacts and his charm and intelligence contributed to his survival.

Eventually after many scrapes and adventures, he saw Jenny ride and was smitten by her. In his usual swashbuckling manner, he asked the director whether there could be "something going" with her. "But no," said the director, "she comes from a respectable family and lives with her father and aunt."[126] The baron kept coming back and Jenny was very much aware of the passionate glances he was giving her. On one occasion, troubled, she fell off her horse, having lost control. People came running to help. So did the baron who got there first and managed to extricate her from under her horse. He rushed to get a military doctor to attend to her. The following day, Rhaden visited her at the hospital. Little by little the baron's charm, his adventurous life, his pleasant conversation, his humor, began to make a strong impression on her. Rhaden, a good observer in such matters, became aware of her sentiments about him. He, in turn, became very serious about her.

---

125   *Ibid.*, 33-34.
126   *Ibid.*, 56, 57.

Meanwhile Jenny's father had made inquiries about Rhaden. They were far from good. Opposition came from all sources, especially from her father. But Jenny was in no way intimidated by Rhaden's past. Rather, she felt it her mission to make him adopt an orderly life. Her father ended by accepting the marriage, although he was still annoyed and returned to Breslau. Rhaden gave up his commission. The members of Rhaden's family also opposed the marriage. What, marry an *ecuyère*? They wanted him to rejoin a regiment. Ignoring the wishes of either parents, they published the marriage bans. Shortly after their marriage they went to Copenhagen where Jenny was to perform at the Circus Busch. Having lost her valuable stallion to Salamonsky, she bought a four year old thoroughbred stallion, Oberon, who also came from the Maas stud farm and had been trained by the famous *écuyer*, le Chevalier Derry. Her success on this horse was instantaneous.

Here, too, she faced problems. The wife of the director wanted to ride Oberon. This was against all protocol, for one does not let another person ride the very horse on whom one has been successful. Jenny's refusal annoyed the directress. Suddenly Oberon fell ill. Director Busch offered to buy him. She accepted, seeing no treachery. Three days later Oberon recovered and was given the name of Farceur.

In Copenhagen, the young couple met several officers, including a certain Lt. de Castensciold, son of the Danish fieldmarshal. He developed a passion for Jenny. Rhaden talked to Castensciold who promised to cease bothering Jenny. The promise was not kept. A remark made by Rhaden about "tiresome fools pestering people" was overheard by the lieutenant, who provoked Rhaden to a duel. Now Castensciold was considered the army's best fencer. This turned out to be the case and Rhaden was wounded in the left temple.

Jenny heard the news just as she was about to perform. She smiled at the audience, as she always did, and performed on her horse. The audience applauded. She then rushed to her husband. She found him surrounded by his fellow officers, head bandaged, a wine glass in his hand, enjoying himself.

Soon they moved to Paris where she performed at the Cirque d'Eté. She received a good press. Articles by a Baron de—, writing under the name of *le Diable boiteux* (the limping devil) wrote several articles praising her performances. On one occasion, the article stated that she rode differently from the other *ecuyères*, riding more dangerously, exposing her life every evening. The article also criticized another *ecuyère*. The reaction was instantaneous. One evening, as Jenny was dismounting and about to remove her foot from the stirrup iron, the lover of this *ecuyère*, the son of an important person, rushed towards her, brandishing a stick in her face. She cried out, frightened. Rhaden saw the scene, dashed forward to apprehend the man, but the attacker ran off and hid in the director's office. Rhaden provoked a duel, but Jenny's attacker rushed off to Versailles, offering money to Jenny in recompense. Rhaden was furious and threw the man sent with the money down the stairs.

Her engagement in Paris continued to flourish and she continued to receive the applause of the many sportsmen attending the circus and of the kindly disposed French public. The Press continued to be very flattering.

The couple went to Turin and then to Milan. In Milan her *tante bien-aimée* (beloved aunt), who had always accompanied her on tour, died. She was grief-stricken.

In Milan she performed at the Circo Mariani. Every night there was a full house and much applause. High society also attended the circus in large numbers and expressed appreciation of the performances of Jenny. This was especially true of a certain count M who wrote love letters to her using "the language of Dante."[127] She ignored the letters. The count became furious when she also ignored his latest most passionate letter. Rhaden fearing another scandal, agreed that she should continue to act as though she had not received this *billet-doux*. Even more furious at this slight, the count came to the circus, blowing on a pea-whistle just as she started her performance in the ring.

Rhaden heard the noise, saw what was happening, and slapped the count. In turn, the count insulted Rhaden when he said that all he was doing was pursuing an "artist." He also questioned the husband's credentials, demanding to see his papers and that they be authenticated by the Russian Embassy. Meanwhile Jenny went off to Asti. Rhaden remained behind to settle the affair, hiring two non-titled lawyers who wrote scathing articles in the press, not only against the count, but also against the two witnesses the count had hired, who then provoked a duel. Rhaden fought first with one whom he wounded in the neck. Then Rhaden fought with the other witness, one of Italy's best duelists. Rhaden was slightly hurt over one eye, his blood blinding him. A "halt" was called, Rhaden lowered his arm, taking a step backwards. At this moment the opponent rushed forward with fury on the defenseless Rhaden, aiming at his heart. Rhaden was hit just under the shoulder. Ignoring the pain, Rhaden took the opponent by the throat and threw him to the ground. Now a legal battle occurred. Although the opponent

---

127 *Ibid.*, 91.

had violated the rules of a gentleman, he was not reprimanded.

At Asti, an accident occurred when a spectator threw a bouquet of flowers at Jenny, which fell at the feet of her horse, frightening him and making him jump forward over the curb between ring and spectators. An old woman was slightly hurt and Jenny had to pay damages. Everything went wrong at Asti. One horse fell ill, another became lame. She was happy to leave and went to Lisbon to perform at the Recreios Coliseo.

One of the movements she had performed frequently, was to make her horse rear in all his height, walk on his hind legs with Jenny leaning back on the horse's croup, her long hair mingling with the horse's tail. This was a dangerous movement because the horse's center of gravity became displaced. In fact, several accidents had occurred but she had been lucky.

It is, I think, appropriate here to discuss Jenny's ability to deal with and control unfamiliar horses. Much of the time, she was performing in the circus, on horses familiar to her. On one occasion in Oporto, Portugal, she witnessed several horsemen trying to ride an obstinate and recalcitrant horse belonging to the Duke of Oporto. All of their attempts ended in being thrown off the horse. She watched for a while and then asked whether she could ride the horse, using her own saddle. She mounted without any hesitation and made the horse execute movements which gave one the impression that he had undergone complete training. This surprised the onlookers.

"You have the most gentle hands in the world," the men shouted.

"Well, gentlemen, try to do likewise. Therein you will find, in all its simplicity, the secret of success,"[128] she answered.

In Madrid Jenny was to perform at the Circo Diaz. Rhaden suddenly complained of pains and a swelling in his chest. An eminent doctor recommended an operation, claiming that otherwise he would live eight days at the most. Rhaden preferred to live eight days rather than undergo an uncertain operation. A purulent abscess soon became visible, was lanced, and within eight days Rhaden was fine. In Malaga they met again with Castensciold of Denmark. They also found him at Clermont-Ferrand. Rhaden asked the director to remove him from the circus, fearing for the life of his wife during one of her performances. Another duel ensued. Castensciold lost and died from his wound. Rhaden was imprisoned.

---

128 *Ibid.*, 162.

Jenny went on to Paris to perform at the Folies-Bergère. The stage there was very difficult and dangerous both to her and the horse. Instead of a ring filled with soil and sawdust, there were wooden planks with an incline upon which was laid a carpet of coco fibers. Then, too, the area was very restrictive for horse and rider to execute the *haute école* movements without the horse slipping or unable to execute his movements.

Moreover there existed the rumors about the duel and her husband's imprisonment. The trial had become a cause célèbre. At the trial the question was raised: was it a voluntary homicide, for if so, it would have given Rhaden five years of prison. Finally he was declared not guilty.

Baronne Jenny de Rhaden on Czardas.

At her first performance at the Folies-Bergère, the hall was filled to capacity. They all came to see the woman who had been the cause of the death of an officer and the imprisonment of her husband. Just prior to her entrance, the commandant of the armed corps of the area, the Marquis de G appeared in gala uniform, surrounded by a group of officers. The public applauded, the ice was broken, and the public became eager to accept her. With each movement executed, the public's applause became more intense.

With this dangerous situation, in which she and her horses were forced to perform aggravated matters, an accident was bound to happen. As the horse got up on his hind legs, Jenny lay back along the horse's croup, the horse slipped and she suddenly found herself under her horse. The audience cried out. However, the intelligent horse got up very slowly and Jenny was not hurt. She got back on her horse and completed her number. A slight contusion, that was all.

There was, of course, a somewhat comic ending to this event. When she returned to the theater the following day, the director received her with smiles and greetings, praising her performance of the previous night, and wanting her to repeat it in its totality, especially "that trick at the end...It was unique, superb," he said. "A trick" she repeated in amazement, "what trick, that was no trick. I can only thank heaven that I came out of it safely."[129] According to Jenny, the director was not happy.

It is perhaps appropriate to describe the complete movements Jenny executed throughout her many performances, as well as those at the Folies-Bergères.

As stated earlier, the space at the Folies-Bergère was restrictive, having a surface of about eight meters. She was forced to perform on a carpet of cocoa fibers as it was not possible to scatter soil or sawdust on sloping wooden planks.

The orchestra began its prelude and Jenny and her horse dashed forward from the wings doing a lançade and a courbette, and then reached the ring curb. It should be noted that there did not exist the usual circular curb between act and orchestra and spectators, making it necessary for her to have her horse in total control. A misstep on the part of the horse and they could both fall into the orchestra. In fact, this was the constant fear of the members of the orchestra, who, at first, had refused to play during her act.

After reaching the edge of the stage, Jenny had her horse do several sidesteps to the right and to the left, then walk. They fell into a fast canter, which was her strength. Then, they executed several voltes in all directions, lead changes at the canter in three, two, and one-tempi, pirouettes, the Spanish walk, then the passage. The latter two movements were especially difficult to execute in such a restrictive space.

She then changed horses. Her stallion jumper, Da Capo, now entered the scene at a hunting gallop which, with the wooden down slope and the fiber carpet, could easily make the horse slide and send them both down on to the orchestra. The performance continued with horse and rider crossing to mid-center, pivoting into a pirouette, the horse then raising himself vertically to his full length, walking on his hind legs, then kneeling in all four corners of the stage. Horse and rider then came to a halt centerstage where the horse reared again as they jumped out of the center.

---

129 *Ibid.*, 148.

Then fences were brought and placed in the center, forming a square. They jumped alternately over each of the four fences. They came to a halt, the horse raised himself and they leaped out of the enclosure.

Parallel bars were now placed along the ring curb over which horse and rider jumped, one after the other. Then came the final movement: the horse reared in all his length, walking on his hind legs, with Jenny lowering her torso until her head touched the horse's croup, horse's tail and Jenny's long hair mingling with each other. The audience, as always, gave a rousing applause.

Jenny appeared once more before the public, but on foot, taking off her *haut-de-forme* and saluting. But that was not all. Her favorite horse, Czardas, also a jumper, appeared riderless at a gallop, knelt down in front of Jenny, and then lay down at her feet. She sat on his side, saluting the public as the curtain fell.

She performed at the Nouveau-Cirque for the season 1890/91 where conditions were better. Everyone tried to make the couple's sojourn pleasant. With the friendship and attentiveness of Baroness W and Madame B, Le Tout Paris opened up to her.

She also performed at the Cirque d'Hiver in 1896 where she repeated her famous movement with her horse rearing, hocks extended, and she leaning far back along the length of her horse's back.

At the Theatre du Châtelet she was asked to play the role of Mazeppa, who, tied to his horse, traverses the steppe at a furious speed.

Conditions began to deteriorate for Jenny and her husband. Rhaden began to suffer from severe chest pains. Czardas became blind, brought about by the intense light of the reflectors. Soon Rhaden died. Jenny became afflicted with heart palpitations, nausea, migraine headaches, and anxiety.

She continued to give performances in Prague, Wiesbaden, London, returned to Italy and Spain, but she had to drag herself to those performances. It was a constant battle between her will power and her deteriorating body. At Nice one day, when awakened by her maid, although the sun was shining into her room, she felt surrounded by a profound darkness. She had become blind. The medical prognosis was that her long-suffering nephritic affliction had provoked a sudden rush of blood to her head, tearing the retina and the optic nerve. Her nervous and over-exited condition and her cardiac spasms made any treatment difficult, if not impossible. At first they believed that this condition was not permanent.

Her director convinced her to perform. Although blind, she believed that she could perhaps continue to earn her living. She preferred to die on a horse as an *ecuyère*, rather than be condemned to a life of desolation.

I entered the *manège* and circled the ring. A minute later I halted in the center. I felt surrounded by an immense crowd, whose noise enveloped me similar to a rushing flood. But I saw absolutely nothing. I could not even see the slightest glimmer of the circus's bright illuminations. I was, so to speak, groping in the dark.

The audience applauded. In my concern, I forgot to thank the audience. I was totally pre-occupied with my horse, giving him all my attention, all my will-power, simply to remain mistress of the situation. I had to count on myself, on the training and the docility of my mount.

I had chosen as mount my white tiger spotted stallion, the blind Czardas, who had, with my direction, always behaved with great docility and obedience. I had no fear, although my powerlessness had overexcited me. Completely blind on a blind horse in the midst of a public that expected wonders and had no concept of my affliction and expected more tours de force! Put yourself in my situation! I simply hoped to do the impossible.[130]

Suddenly Jenny realized that Czardas was resisting her. Perhaps his sensitive nature made him aware that she had no real control over him. He refused to move. She then used her crop. "Troubled, trembling with fear, he began to move backwards, as though he felt an abyss in front of him."[131]

A terrible battle ensued between rider and horse. The horse then bounded forward. The audience now sensed that something was wrong and cried out in terror, making matters worse. She fell from the horse and hit one of the columns. She became comatose and remained so for a week.

Jenny was moved to Paris while the horses she loved had to remain in Cannes. During the move, one of her horses was hit by a tram and killed. Czardas, who had contributed to her first triumph in Riga and had been her downfall during her last performance, was shot. She will always remember him with gratitude.

She thinks of the past, her former triumphs, the enthusiastic applause of the public, and wonders whether this mournful desolation

---

130 *Ibid.*, 213-214

131 *Ibid*, 214.

was worth it. Would she have done it all over again? Indeed, she relives it all in her memory and her autobiography.
Baronesse de Rhaden died in 1921.

In *Écuyer*s and *Ecuyères*, le Baron de Vaux, one of the few horsemen to discuss the talents of women riders of the nineteenth century, says that Jenny de Rhaden was an outstanding *ecuyère* doing *haute école*, executing pirouettes, lead changes at the canter, the Spanish walk, and other movements with great finesse; "although it was Germanic equitation, it was nonetheless, equitation."[132] But, Vaux asks himself, why did she have to resort to these acrobatic stunts? Just to get bravos from the spectators? But this denotes courage, not talent. She could easily have dispensed with these stunts, for she was an excellent horsewoman. She rode well, had a good seat, and had her horse well in hand. If only she had rid herself of these stunts, she would have been an outstanding *ecuyère*.

Ah, yes! But le Baron de Vaux never heard the director ask Jenny to repeat the finale of one of her performances when she found herself under her horse and escaped injury because her horse had raised himself quietly. And the disappointment of the director when Jenny told him that this was not a trick and that she was only glad to have escaped serious injury.

Jenny de Rhaden inspired the film Elvira Madigan, although the film dealt with a tightrope walker rather than an *ecuyère* performing *haute école*. Jenny also inspired Toulouse-Lautrec, whose drawings of the circus became famous. This collection of thirty-nine drawings, entitled Cirque, was executed in 1899 when he was incarcerated in a sanatorium in Neuilly and evokes personalities of the past: Ernest Molier, Baroness de Rhaden, the bear Caviar, and many other well-known artists of the circus world. Lautrec's drawings, executed from memory, brought back some aspects of the past to an afflicted man. Although a troubled prisoner in a sanatorium, Lautrec's Cirque denotes his continued lucidity and his artistic power. It is a triumph over his affliction and incarceration through his art and his memory.

In a sense one can say that the blind *ecuyère* and the ill incarcerated artist were both victims of an all-encompassing darkness. Yet both were able to find release from this darkness: Lautrec through his art and his memories; Jenny de Rhaden, who, through her autobiography was able to relive the past and her triumphs.

---

132 Baron de Vaux, *Écuyers et Ecuyères*, 213.

CHAPTER IX:
ADELE DROUIN, DIANE DUPONT, MARGUERITE DUDLEY AND BLANCHE ALLARTY-MOLIER

ADELE DROUIN

Adèle Drouin received her training from Maxime Gaussen, de Corbie, and Victor Franconi. She first appeared at the Hippodrome de l'Alma in 1865 or 66.

According to critics she was a pretty woman of medium height, had a "marvelous bosom" as Vaux puts it, and was charming in the saddle. Her seat and posture were exceptional. Together with Monsieur de Corbie she initially rode the jumpers of Versailles, (horses who execute the school jumps—*sauts d'école*) trained by Maxime Gaussen, to execute the high airs typical of the former École de Versailles. These horses apparently were so heavy and harsh in their jumps that the men who tried them out could only stay on them with difficulty, even though they used special training saddles (selles à pìquer). But Adèle Drouin was able to stay on. She was never displaced. She was one of the few *ecuyères* who could equal, if not better, many of the outstanding *écuyer*s.

Soon Adèle learned how to work with her horse without a bridle. This horse was called Diane and had been trained by Faverot de Kerbrech.

Faverot de Kerbrech was first trained by his father, General Baron Faverot who had been a pupil of le Chevalier d'Abzac of the *Manège* de Versailles (École de Versailles). Faverot de Kerbrech and General L'Hotte were two of François Baucher's favorite pupils. Faverot continued much of the work of Baucher, that is, the later part of Baucher's work known as his "*deuxième maniere*" (second manner), and which he entitled *Dressage méthodique du cheval de selle d'après les derniers enseignements de Baucher, recueillis par un de ses élèves* [*Methodical Dressage of the Riding Horse*…,Xenophon Press, 2010]. This work was published in 1891, twenty years after the death of the master.

Faverot was an outstanding horseman whose aim in training the horse was lightness. And lightness was one important ingredient that made it possible for Adèle Drouin to make her horse, Diane, execute many *haute école* movements without a bridle.

According to Vaux, to obtain the training of a horse without a bridle, it is necessary to execute what is known as the "*arrêt à toutes les allures*"[133] (the halt at all the gaits). Initially the horse must still wear the bridle, but the reins are placed around his neck at the walk. By means of the crop, one touches the horse lightly on the neck. Simultaneously or immediately thereafter, one stops and picks up the reins, but only briefly, in the other hand. One repeats these movements six, ten, even twenty times until the horse halts only when he is touched on the neck with the crop. Of course, when the horse performs well, one caresses him or gives him a treat.

Adèle Drouin.

One continues to repeat these movements until the horse stops as soon as he either feels the crop on his neck or, better still, senses that the crop will touch his neck.

When the work is successful one goes on to the trot and then the canter. The work is the same for the trot and the canter, as well as for the reinback.

Thus the reins are replaced by the crop and one can achieve such movements as slowing down, the halt, and the reinback. When the horse successfully accomplishes the "halt at all the gaits" the bridle can be removed. Eventually one tries to achieve the same movements by means of one's voice.

After the Hippodrome de l'Alma burned down, Adèle performed at the Cirque des Champs-Elysées. Whether working with or without a bridle, her typical performances, were as follows:

Adèle entered the *manège* at a fast canter, looking magnificent on her

---

133   Baron de Vaux, *Écuyers et Ecuyères*, 130.

splendid horse, halted, gave the salute of the *ecuyère*, executed the reinback, and then, still moving backwards, executed a figure eight.

She then executed pirouettes to the right and to the left. Then came the pas d'école, one of the most magnificent airs of *haute école*, and Adèle's horse actually seemed to float. She then proceeded to do a figure eight, then moved on to successive lead changes at the canter. Then came the Spanish walk on the right leg, then the left leg, intermingled with halts. Then the horse and rider departed at the gallop, intermingled with flying lead changes and instantaneous halts. Horse and rider then executed the piaffe and the passage, the Spanish trot, then an extended canter, and an immediate halt in the center of the *manège*. Executing a reinback, Adèle rapidly left the *manège*.

But her little mare, Diane, was able to perform these movements without a bridle. Never before had spectators of a circus witnessed a horse and rider perform *haute école* without a bridle. This feat was first accomplished by Adèle at the Hippodrome in 1868 where she performed a complete programme with neither bridle nor bit. Diane was able to execute perfect flying changes on circles at every stride, at one tempo and at two tempi. She also executed perfectly two, three, or more successive flying changes at every stride. All the while, Adèle used her hands and leg imperceptibly and with great finesse.

Diane piaffed well in place, maintaining at all times excellent cadence, rounded movements of the hips, and equal suspension of front legs and hind legs. The horse then moved slightly forward with the necessary impulsion to enter into the passage, moving two or three inches at each stride. Diane's movements were rounded, legs were graceful and cadenced, the trot was elevated and slow; while movement at the rear was less elevated it still retained its springiness.

Then the horse returned to the piaffe and entered into the backward trot, but the movement was not much more than two to three inches at each stride.

It should be mentioned that working with a horse without a bridle or bit requires considerable skill and tact on the part of the trainer, whether it is in preparation for a performance in a ring or *manège* or for the outdoors.

In the nineteenth century, an outstanding horseman, Commandant Rousselet, soft-spoken, wise, and gentle with both pupil and horse, was *écuyer en Chef* at the École de Cavalerie. Rousselet was able to handle successfully, with only a silk string, a strong-willed horse that had the bad habit of carrying off his riders and unseating them.

According to Halperson, another *ecuyère*, Mathilde Monnet, who, in the 1840s performed in the Cirque Olympique and in the

1850s in the Circus Renz, also accomplished this feat when she rode one of her horses without saddle or bridle.[134]

In the 1950s Fredy Knie, Sr. performed the same feat, using neither bridle nor saddle on his horse, Rablo. His son, Fredy Knie, Jr. repeated his father's performance on his Andalusian, Parzi, executing flying lead changes, pirouettes, the polka, and the Spanish walk and trot.[135]

DIANE DUPONT

As a young girl Diane Dupont had wanted to be a dramatic actress and went to le Theatre du Gymnase, where she was successful. She was also an enterprising outdoor rider. Charles Zidler, who was director of the Hippodrome de l'Alma at the time, met her frequently in the Bois de Boulogne. One day he told her that she rode very well and predicted that in six months she would be performing at the Hippodrome. The young woman laughed, thanked Zidler for his compliment, and went on her way.

The Hippodrome de l'Alma, which had succeeded the earlier Hippodrome de l'Etoile, was an oval-shaped arena whose activities included horse racing, chariot racing, carrousels, obstacle jumping, equestrian pantomimes and other spectacles. In the center of the oval, with paths leading from its four sides, a ring for *haute école* performances was situated. Many famous *ecuyères*, in addition to performing *haute école* at the Hippodrome, also raced their horses, jumped them over obstacles, even participated in chariot-racing as did Elise Petzold and Diane Dupont.

Shortly after this exchange between the future *ecuyère* and Zidler, Diane Dupont heard of a little mare that was for sale. She went to see her, found her perfect, and bought her. With such a perfect horse she felt that she should take lessons from a competent teacher and thus perfect her seat and posture.

She asked James Fillis to give her lessons which he was willing to do. For several months Diane worked hard to acquire that perfect seat and posture. Zidler, aware that she was taking lessons from Fillis, was so certain of success that he offered her an engagement at the Hippodrome. Diane was later also a pupil of le Comte de Montigny, a former *écuyer* of the École de Cavalerie of Saumur, a man who had devoted his whole life to equitation. He had also written several books

---

134 Josef von Halperson, *Das Buch vom Zirkus*, 149.

135 Monica J. Renevey, *Le Grand Livre du Cirque*, Vol. II, 52.

on equitation, one of them being *L'Equitation des dames*.

Diane enjoyed the sessions with Fillis. In fact, she found such pleasure in equitation that she gave up the idea of returning to the theater, finding equitation more rewarding and amusing than acting. She therefore accepted Zidler's offer.

In 1884 Diane appeared for the first time at the Hippodrome with Dollar, a horse she had bought from Elise Petzold, who was retiring from the circus. Dollar's training had already been completed with Elise and his work on two tracks was known to be irreproachable, as were his flying changes.

Diane also bought Froufrou, a jumper who had twice been a winner at the Concours Hippique in 1884 and a winner at an obstacle jumping competition in 1885. Despite the fact that Froufrou had difficulty complying with the demands of *manège* riding, and, above all, circus riding, he ended being a "finished" horse, that is, he became a disciplined, supple, and light horse, performing with grace and lightness.

Vaux considers it remarkable that Dupont was able to triumph over a horse that had originally been trained for a different discipline. How did she triumph over this horse's resistances, he asks himself? The answer is really quite simple. When Froufrou tried to resist, he encountered a gentle but firm hand, a hand which made him perform the movements required. Thus little by little the horse began to get used to obeying a will that was greater than his own and followed willingly the commands given him.

Indeed, finesse, elegance, and tact are indispensable. A rider must never use violence whether it is training a horse or performing in the ring. For if grace, elegance, finesse, and tact are replaced by force and violence, any performance becomes unseemly, even ugly and painful to watch. According to Vaux, Diane Dupont had all the qualities that contribute to making a horse disciplined, supple, light, and, yet, energetic. She had skill, patience, and, above all, she had equestrian tact, so indispensable to the training of a horse. She was, in short, an *ecuyère* of great stature.

Like many of the *ecuyères* mentioned, Diane Dupont trained her horse herself, thus becoming aware of the qualities and the defects of the horse upon whom she must impose certain exercises and upon whom she must ultimately depend. By doing so, and by learning to observe him carefully, she came to know how much she could ask of him and how to regulate the exercises to the extent of his strength and his aptitude. She also knew that she should not ask too much of him. Nor should she ask too little.

Dupont had, indeed, acquired this irreproachable seat and posture that she had initially sought; her aids were imperceptible, and the lightest pressure of her fingers sufficed to communicate with all of her horses.

According to Vaux, Diane Dupont did not compress her horse as many of the *ecuyères* sometimes did. Furthermore, once her horse was set in motion, he went forward and upward with lightness and suppleness. Every movement was executed with the greatest of ease; every movement was always correct and graceful.

Once mounted, Diane was sure of herself and of her horse. She never hesitated and her horse, knowing her well and having confidence in her, would do whatever she wanted him to do and, so to speak, go to the end of the world if she did not tell him to stop. Vaux ends his discussion of Dupont by saying that of all the *ecuyères* performing in the circus, Diane Dupont was one of the most outstanding, and, with the exception of Anna Fillis, no one could equal her talent. In the final analysis, says Vaux, she can, indeed, be considered an elegant and harmonious interpreter of the French Classical School of Equitation. Vaux' only criticism is that she makes certain concessions to this profession, of which I am only too aware. I know that this is necessary when one is dealing with equitation in the circus, an art that addresses itself to every type of spectator, for in the circus, one must charm, astonish, dazzle, in order to get from the spectators all the bravos one can. For that reason one is inclined to misrepresent traditional *haute école*, force one's horse to execute the Spanish walk, make him kneel as though he were a learned performing dog. I do not call these tricks, art, I call them acrobatics, and I would be pleased to show Mlle. Dupont how this slope can only lead downwards and that she should avoid it.[136]

Yet, despite all these tricks, Vaux is forced to concede that Dupont and her horse worked harmoniously and elegantly together, especially when they limited themselves to executing *haute école* movements.

As was usual with many *ecuyères*, Diane Dupont traveled with her horses to perform in Berlin, Vienna, London's Covent Garden, and Brussels. Everywhere she and her horses went, they were enthusiastically applauded. She returned to Paris to perform at the Cirque d'Eté and the Nouveau Cirque. At the latter circus she also presented horses performing at liberty.

---

136   Vaux, *Écuyers et Ecuyères*, 168.

MARGUERITE DUDLEY

La petite Dudley, as she was called, made her entree at the Cirque des Champs-Elysées. Long before becoming an *ecuyère*, she had the habit of coming to the circus almost daily to observe Emilie Loisset rehearse with her horse. As was the case with Elise Petzold, she, too, was infatuated or, as Vaux expresses it, haunted by the circus and equestrian activities. Unlike the Petzold family who sent poor Elise to a convent, the family of Marguerite was accommodating and granted her wish.

After several months of rigorous training, she went through the regular steps that almost all beginning *ecuyères* have to go through: the school quadrilles, then on to group rehearsals executing *haute école*. The acute eye and professionalism of Charles Franconi noticed Marquerite's energy, her close application and perseverance, and her elegant horsemanship. Soon she was selected from the group with the intention of shaping her into an *ecuyère* of *haute école*. "Today," says Vaux, "Mlle Dudley can take her place among the great *ecuyères*. Her horse, Moskowa, with whom she presented herself, is proof of her excellence."[137]

Marguerite began performing with Moskowa at the Cirque d'Eté. This horse was able to execute all the *haute école* movements with remarkable clarity and precision. Furthermore, Marguerite used her aids, that is, her spur and her crop, very sparingly and yet succeeded in making her horse execute lead changes at various strides; the Spanish walk and trot were executed while retaining the necessary impulsion and support. In short all the difficulties a young equestrian debutante faces, were easily and excellently handled.

Her seat and posture were excellent, her torso so correct, blending so well with the body of her horse that she almost gave the impression of being a centauress. She exhibited the necessary finesse and tact. "In a word," says Vaux " she is an *ecuyère* of incontestable superiority, the ideal elegant *amazone*."[138]

Le Roux relates a charming little story that demonstrates the affinity, even love, an *ecuyère* can have for a special horse, a trait that has been mentioned here quite frequently. Le Roux was observing Marguerite Dudley jumping with her horse, Moskowa, over an obstacle at the Cirque d'Eté. Moskowa was a stallion of Slavic lineage, elegant, possessing an exemplary conformation. He was, as Le Roux describes his secret disposition, "full of revolts, impetuousness passion, violence,

---

137 *Ibid.*, 183.

138 *Ibid.*, 183.

but clothed in a faint gentleness, submerged with pliability."[139] It was clear to Le Roux that Marguerite loved all her horses, but that she had a special relationship with this particular stallion as opposed to her other horse, Regent, a handsome Polish horse, "who was more reliable than his comrade, more loyal, more courageous, vigorous, but who hid his loving nature behind a military appearance and the correct stiffness of an officer."[140] Marguerite admitted to Le Roux that she was not being fair to Regent, "but what do you want! Moskowa and I, we love each other." And explains Le Roux with acumen:

There you have the secret of *haute école* as in everything else. Mere habit and skill do not suffice, love is essential. It is through the love expressed by little hands that flatter their necks that stallions are generous with the bursts of energy that exhaust them, through love that they humiliate themselves, that they kneel down. Yet, as far as I am concerned, there is no spectacle that is more grandiose and, in general, more spiritual, no triumph that is more admirable than will power over force, mind over matter."[141]

This little revelation related by Le Roux and the affinity that Marguerite had for one special horse rather than for another, can perhaps explain the preference many *ecuyères* had for their particular horse.

As it had happened to Emilie Loisset, Marguerite Dudley also experienced a similar accident, almost bringing her career to an end. This occurred in 1889 during a rehearsal.

She had just jumped over a fence and was going into a Spanish trot, when her Russian horse, Dvornick, quickly began to go backwards and at one bound, went up on his hocks, falling over with great violence on top of Marguerite. Those nearby went to her aid to try to extricate the poor girl who was suffocating under the weight of the horse. It took them several minutes to get her out from under him. Hurt and unconscious, they picked her up. They could not help but think of poor Emilie who had never made it. But what had killed Emilie, saved the life of Marguerite. While the fork of the saddle had perforated the abdomen of Emilie, in this instance the very fork, situated to the left of the saddle, saved her from being squashed by the horse, which, luckily, had fallen to the right.

---

139   Hughes Le Roux, *Les Jeux du cirque et la vie foraine*, 126.
140   *Ibid.*, 126.
141   *Ibid.*, 127-128.

When three months later, Marguerite returned to the ring, the public gave her a standing ovation, proof of the esteem which they had for the young *ecuyère* and an expression of delight at her return to performing *haute école* for their pleasure.

Marguerite also introduced to her repertoire horses at liberty. She first began with her horse, Regent. Marguerite, on foot, lunge whip in hand, with Regent, bridled and saddled, but unmounted, made the horse execute all the *manège* airs, including pirouettes, lead changes, jumping over fences, and other *haute école* movements that are generally performed mounted. "This innovation" says Vaux, "broke the monotony that sometimes happens with *haute école*."[142]

Soon Marguerite became as adept at handling the lunge whip as she had formerly handled the riding whip, achieving wonderful results in this new type of work. Vaux tells us that as he writes this description of her, she has at the moment six horses performing at liberty and that she uses the lunge whip with great skill, touching the haunches of one horse gently to make him go forward, or the shoulder of another to make him go backwards.

BLANCHE ALLARTY-MOLIER

Blanche Allarty is closely connected with the Cirque Molier whose director was Ernest Molier. This circus was a privately owned circus, a *"cirque mondain"* put at the disposal of amateurs, usually friends and acquaintances of Molier who vied for the honor of performing not only *haute école* or equine acrobatics, but also other circus acts. The Cirque Molier was situated in the Rue Bénouville, right next to the Bois de Boulogne and formed part of Molier's *hotel particulier*. The circus had an excellent ring and a large hall to seat the spectators.

The opening night occurred 21 March 1880. Friends, relatives, and acquaintances were invited. The invitation read: "We will do a little equitation, a little acrobatics and then we will eat tripe *à la Bénouville*."[143] The seats were not the most comfortable, but Molier had tried to make the atmosphere more festive by creating a Spanish motif. Present were the upper bourgeoisie and aristocracy of the horse world: le Prince de Sagan, le Prince de Chenay, le Baron d'Orgeval, le Duc de Morny, le Comte d'Osmond, etc. To enliven the evening, professional *ecuyères* such as Fanny Lehmann, a delicate

---

142 *Ibid.*, 185.

143 Adrian, *Histoire illustrée des cirques parisiens*, 186.

Blanche Allarty-Molier doing the Capriole on d'Artagnan.

rider, yet energetic, always in harmony with her horse, known as the Sarah Bernhardt of equitation, and a few others, were asked to participate; so was the actress Alice Lavigne included among the amateurs of the Cirque Molier. Men such as le Comte de Beauregard, le Comte de Maulde performed equestrian acts; le Comte Hubert de la Rochefoucauld and others performed at the trapeze and the fixed bar. The evening was so successful that it was agreed that there would be a repeat performance the following year. Indeed, each year the Cirque Molier gave its annual spectacle until 1933. To these yearly performances Le Tout-Paris came. Even the *demi-monde*, and the *horizontales de grande marque* were received.

While a certain amount of frivolity animated these evenings, the enthusiasm of the members of high society, and the enthusiasm and skill engendered by Molier himself, gave the Cirque Molier a special animation and cachet. The original ideas and the talent that came to the fore, gave the Cirque Molier a certain stamp of distinction.

Even Molier's acrobats, jugglers and clowns came from Le Tout-Paris. They were mostly amateurs, performing their acts for fun and doing them well, capable of competing with the professional *écuyer*s and *ecuyère*s, acrobats, and clowns.

The women also came from Le Tout-Paris, those who wanted to

perform and show off their skills as horsewomen, as did many of the *ecuyères* performing in the circus on a professional basis. Molier was in no way in awe of those titled amateur performers. They, too, were given broom and shovel with which to pick up manure.

Hughes Le Roux makes an interesting comment in *Les Jeux du Cirque et la vie foraine* when he compares the amateur circus artist and the professional one. "Whereas the acrobat tried to become a man of the world, the man of the world was becoming an excellent acrobat...The gentleman has vacated his seat in the circus to show himself on the *panneau* or on the trapeze."[144]

Molier trained many young women who eventually performed in the circuses of Paris and other capitals of Europe. Many of his trainees performed attired as men, for example, Louise Lankaster dressed as Louis XIII and Blanche Allarty as an *écuyer* of Saumur.

Blanche Allarty was thirteen years old when she came to Molier for riding lessons. Her father was also an amateur horseman. Molier immediately realized that she possessed the temperament ideal for equitation, for she was supple, agile, robust, enterprising, even daring. Above all, she was passionate about everything that had to do with horses and horsemanship.

She made her debut at the Franconi circus, that is, at the Cirque des Champs-Elysées, specializing primarily in vaulting and equestrian acrobatics. She also performed a very difficult acrobatic act on horseback known as *"voltige à la Richard."* Never before had an *ecuyère* performed this feat. *"Voltige à la Richard"* was named after its creator Davis Richard, a North American, who was killed while executing this act. The horse moves without a saddle, there is not even a *panneau* available. Neither is the horse bridled. The rider, running close to the side of the horse, jumps over hurdles as the horse jumps. Then the horse continues to jump over more hurdles while the rider stands on him.

Allarty soon became one of France's most famous and admired *ecuyère* of *haute école*, often attired in the elegant *amazone* mode, riding side saddle, or dressed in male apparel, riding astride. She also executed not only equestrian acrobatics but also trapeze acrobatics.

She was one of those *ecuyères* who trained their own horses believing that the more contact one had with one's horse, the greater grew mutual trust and dependency.

Her special horse was d'Artagnan whom she trained herself and who, due to her own energy, passion, agility, and abilities, was,

---

144   Hughes le Roux, *ibid.*, 229.

himself, agile and energetic, always in disciplined motion, always executing the regular *haute école* movements or the high airs with vigor and brilliance. She was one of the few *ecuyères* dressed in *amazone* attire who was able to make her amazing horse, d'Artagnan, execute simultaneously a disciplined *lançade* and a *cabriole*.

When she performed in New York, the press and spectators nicknamed her "Centauress." Ernest Molier was considered a Centaur. There is a delightful drawing in Adrian's book, *Histoire Illustrée des Cirques parisiens* presenting Molier as a centaur, crop in his hand and *haut-de-forme* on his head.

Blanche Allarty-Molier doing the Cabrade on d'Artagnan.

In his book, *L'Equitation et le cheval* published in 1911 Molier explains to the reader why, when he completed the riding sessions, he asked his pupils to ride astride. Many of his pupils became noted *ecuyères*.

Since riding astride for a woman would have been received poorly by any passerby, causing a commotion or even provoking a scandal, Molier was obliged to have his *ecuyères* ride in the woods at night by moonlight.

Riding astride was for a long time, especially with the rise of the bourgeoisie, considered improper and also inelegant. Due to woman's physical make-up, so it was believed, riding astride was considered damaging to her health and body. Yet, apparently this was not considered the case with the "*grandes dames*" of the past, as for example Diane de Poitiers, Anne de Beaujeu,

Blanche Allarty-Molier - *Haute école à la française* - doing the piaffe.

daughter of Louis XI, Queen Isabella of Spain and Castille, Margaret of Austria, and many other court ladies, who rode astride if they wished, often preferring it, in that they considered it more convenient and safer, especially if they hunted or where involved in warfare, as were Joan of Arc and Queen Isabella of Spain and Castille.

Molier was convinced that an *ecuyère* worthy of the name, should also be able to ride astride. However, Molier felt, that riding astride was not necessary if one wanted only to perform *haute école*. If one insisted on riding astride one should then wear a *jupeculotte* that reached down to the ankles. One problem with the use of the sidesaddle is that due to the fact that both rider's legs are on the near-side, it results that neither rider nor saddle are properly balanced. Even moving the pommel a few inches to the left of the center line, as was done to remedy the problem, did not help much. Another problem that arises is that since the left leg does not rest solidly in the stirrup iron, but is left more or less dangling, the stirrup is not of great use. These problems, however, as Molier points out, in no way restricted the *ecuyère* from doing *haute école* in the circus ring or the *manège*.

Another interesting point with respect to the use of the sidesaddle[145] is, that a horse ridden sidesaddle should frequently, so to speak, be rebalanced by having someone ride him astride, for the horse can become one-sided. Likewise, as Victor Franconi pointed out, the circus horse working in a ring and putting his weight primarily on his inside bipeds, has to be frequently walked in a straight line to protect him from the possibility of limping. Nevertheless, Blanche Allarty (who became Molier's wife), Yola de Nyss, and many others trained by Molier, rode sidesaddle as an *amazone* or astride, depending whether they were performing *haute école* or very demanding equestrian acrobatics.

Blanche Allarty-Molier on Mustapha doing the cabrade (courbette).

It should be noted that some of the photographs introduced here demonstrate astonishingly well the talent of both Blanche Allarty and d'Artagnan.

To quote le Baron de Vaux,."..generally speaking, a woman, when she acquires the taste and the passion [for equitation], ordinarily shows herself superior to a man; I say this at the risk of wounding the selfesteem of men."[146] Blanche Allarty, with the attributes she possessed, her motivation, her equestrian tact, was

---

145   Josef von Halperson, *ibid.*, 147.

146   Vaux, *ibid.*, 141.

able to bring about this harmony between horse and rider, this interdependence and perfect correspondence of the wills of both woman and horse.

It should not be forgotten that, according to Adrian, it was thanks to Ernest Molier and Blanche Allarty-Molier "the horse retained, within a certain milieu, his prestige, despite all the mechanical devices that were eclipsing him."[147]

---

[147] Adrian, *ibid.*, 188.

CHAPTER X:
EPILOGUE OF FOUR CONTEMPORARY *Écuyeres*:

KATJA SCHUMANN BINDER
CATHERINE DURAND HENRIQUET
ELOISE SCHWARZ KING
GERALDINE KATHARINA KNIE

KATJA SCHUMANN BINDER

Somewhat belatedly, I decided to add an Epilogue to include contemporary *ecuyères* performing in the circus and in competitive dressage, especially in the Musical Kür. I did so in order to show that the tradition of performing *haute école* and equestrian acrobatics either in a bona fide Classical circus, or single-handedly in a circus related environment, or performing *haute école* movements in dressage competition, especially in the musical Kür, continues to exist among a number of *ecuyères*.

Included are two *ecuyères* performing in regular circuses, Géraldine Katharina Knie of the National Swiss Circus of the Gebrueder Knie Cirkus, and Katja Schumann of the Big Apple Circus. I have included Eloise King because, although not part of a bona fide circus, she performs before small groups in Southern California, a mixture of *haute école* and equestrian acts that occur in a regular circus. I have included Catherine Henriquet because she competes in the Musical Kür (she was France's champion in 1993) as well as in regular dressage competition. The musical Kür is a competitive event that is not too far removed from a performance in the circus: music, costumes, and a certain amount of freedom to go beyond the regular prescribed movements.

I realize that there are other *ecuyères* I should have included in this Epilogue, *ecuyères* such as Maud Gruss of the Alexis Gruss Cirque à l'Ancienne of Paris. A reviewer of the September 2000 issue of the *King Pole* magazine pointed out that in recent years Maud Gruss presents the "Courier of Saint Petersburg" with anywhere between fourteen to seventeen horses passing between the two horses she straddles, with the horses then moving forward in twos or threes. Maud's father, Alexis Gruss, stands in the center of the ring, controlling the performance, as does Fredy Knie, Jr. when Géraldine performs in the same equestrian act.

CATHERINE DURAND HENRIQUET

In an article entitled "An Iberian in International Competition" that Catherine Henriquet wrote for Andalusian magazine a few years ago, she said: "It all began when I was sixteen years of age and we had just moved to Bailly. I was walking my dog and discovered that there were horses in the vicinity."

Indeed, the master of the establishment, who invited Catherine Durand to observe the horses as they were being worked, was none other than *Maître* Michel Henriquet, *écuyer par excellence*, teacher and trainer of horses, writer of books on equitation, a disciple of *Maître* Nuno Oliveira. (Michel Henriquet also became Catherine's husband).

And so began the birth and the long process of Catherine's new passion and her discovery of *haute école* equitation.

But Catherine still had to complete the *lycée*, obtain her *bachot*, and study the art and science of medicine. When time permitted, she studied the art and science of horsemanship. Above all she became acquainted with the Iberian horse, the Lusitano and Andalusian.

At first Catherine was put to breaking (or perhaps one should say gentling) young horses which contributed to giving her a solid seat. She also began to be acquainted with the famous dictum of François Baucher which belongs to his "second manner": "Hand without legs, legs without hand.."

She soon learned from *Maître* Henriquet how to teach a horse to move correctly forward, in a straight line, to bend him properly on curved lines, and to give him a sense of the various cadences that is so necessary in accustoming him to the ascending and descending transitions within each of the three gaits.

After a few years, Catherine graduated beyond the basic work and began to ride horses that had been trained by *Maître* Henriquet; she executed the shoulder in, the half pass and other movements, and eventually began to train horses herself in the execution of all the school movements.

Meanwhile Catherine completed her medical studies and began to practice medicine. It should be noted that Catherine retained her amateur status. Indeed, Henriquet, himself, kept his amateur status and continued to be occupied with his own profession, namely, law and business.

Catherine was immediately entranced by the Iberian horses in *Maître* Henriquet's establishment, a breed not yet well-known in France or, for that matter, in other parts of the world. For the Iberian horse, due to his conformation, his temperament, his generosity, his natural suppleness, his ability to discern what the rider wants of him, or, as Catherine puts it, "a horse who is with the rider," is the ideal horse for achieving the *ramener* and the *rassembler*. In short, the Iberian horse is known for acquiring, without difficulty, and possessing almost innately, that lightness which all serious riders seek for their horses. While much of her equestrian formation was received through Michel Henriquet, many other *écuyers en Chef* from the many famous riding academies who visited the Henriquet establishment, imparted their expertise to Catherine: Thautcher of the Spanish Riding School of Vienna counselled her with respect to executing the levade with her horse Orphée; Borba of the Portuguese School of Equestrian Art perfected her piaffe; Alvaro Domecq of the Royal School of Jerez, another famous horseman, imparted to her the vitality of combat equitation. But it was Colonel Carde, former *Écuyer en Chef* of the Cadre Noir, who talked Catherine into riding competitively. It is interesting to note that Catherine took to competition without any difficulty, as it gave her the possibility of exhibiting the training of her horses. This new aspect of Catherine's

Catherine riding Orphée, executing the piaffe.

equestrian formation, namely, competitive involvement, presented a certain number of difficulties due to the fact that she was competing with a horse who was atypical and with whom the international judges were unfamiliar. There were also the preconceived ideas that people, including judges, had (and still have) with respect to the Iberian horse: to many he is gaudy or flashy. Moreover, Catherine, through *Maître* Henriquet, a disciple of *Maître* Nuno Oliveira, and through direct instruction from Oliveira himself, found it difficult to participate in elementary competition in that her horse had already been *rassemblé*. In other words, the natural flexibility of the Lusitano horse counted against her—"Orphee was too flowing" it was often said. Thus she had to teach herself and Orphée how to maintain, for several minutes, a constant cadence on inside tracks as well as on curves at a very collected and a very extended trot or canter.

Soon Catherine graduated from elementary competition to the Grand Prix.

Orphée, at the age of eight, was able to execute with distinction all the airs required for this competition. But it was at the age of twelve, the year of the Olympic Games in Barcelona, that Orphée reached his best level. For now, Orphée, while better channeled, nevertheless preserved lightness and impulsion, traits that give to the *haute école* horse its cachet.

Catherine Henriquet on Orphée, executing the levade.

It was at a reception during the Olympic Games trials in Barcelona that Williams, the judge from New Zealand, and Mechlen, the German judge, told Catherine to relax for "we have already proven to you that we have made an effort to understand the Iberian horse."

It is interesting when one notes that during her participation in European international competitions, Catherine received marks from the various judges that were quite contradictory.

Quite obviously many of the judges did not quite know how to react to the appearance of an Iberian horse on the rectangles of the European scene. The suppleness and the natural brilliance of the Iberian horse denote a clear contrast with the athletic strength and the somewhat rigid gaits that the horses of northern Europe possess

In 1993 Catherine won, with Orphée, the championship of France in the musical Kür. Above all, Orphée, by bringing together all those exceptional traits mentioned earlier, and due to the skill, passion, and energy of Catherine (who, due to her profession, can only devote a few hours a day to equitation), made it possible for him to be classified among the twenty-five best horses in the world.

Catherine has also worked with Orphée's half-brother

"*Galope sur place*" as the Marquis de la Bigne.

Spartacus. After participating in a Grand Prix International, Spartacus qualified with a grade that Orphée had never been able to achieve. Unfortunately, due to acute tendinitis, Catherine was forced to interrupt his training. This made her participation with Spartacus in the Olympic games in Atlanta impossible.

However, Catherine continued to compete internationally and continued to make a name for herself in many of these competitions.

Since 1995 Catherine and *Maître* Henriquet began training Trakehners. Their goal was to choose horses who had a natural equilibrium, who were sensitive and had good gaits. Unfortunately, no Iberian horses could be found to fit these criteria.

However, these traits were found in the Trakehner, that is, in the type of Trakehner who goes back to pre-World War II and who can now be found mostly in Russia. Today's German Trakehner, that is, the breed now found in Germany, has been bred with Thoroughbreds and lacks the criteria delineated earlier. But the breed belonging to pre-WWII possesses the very traits ideal for competition: an aptitude for being easily *rassemblé*, for being able to *piaffer* and execute the passage without difficulty, as well as to execute all the other *haute école* movements with ease.

Catherine is now working with an eight year old Trakehner, classed Grand Prix, and an eight year old Hanoverian. Both are fully able to execute all the prescribed *haute école* movements. However,

Catherine on Spartacus performing a passage.

they are not yet ready to put the movements together, that is, they are not yet ready to put the movements in the prescribed sequence. The sequence of movements, that is, to pass from one movement to the other for Grand Prix, are devised to be expressly difficult for the competitor. It is, for example, especially difficult for an as yet inexperienced horse to be asked to go from a flexed movement to a straight movement or vice versa.

However, the Henriquets have not neglected the Iberian horse. They were given two Iberian horses by a Portuguese breeder, who was thanking them for promoting the Iberian horse. Catherine has been training them since January 2000. While both have good gaits, she intends to keep the four year old who is strong, very flexed and has a good equilibrium.

I was especially interested in Catherine's approach to the Musical Kür since it comes closest to *haute école* executed in the circus.

In the regular dressage competition, the sequence of movements is imposed upon the rider, whereas in the Musical Kür one is relatively free with respect to the sequence in which prescribed movements are executed. The use of music and the choice of costume makes the Musical Kür more interesting to the average spectator and is more media oriented. However, when I asked about the execution of the *pas d'école* or the *pas espagnol*, Catherine told me that the former was not accepted in competition—in fact, it was considered a defect, and the latter movement was considered too exuberant; the extended walk or the collected walk was what the horse was allowed to execute.

While in the Musical Kür the sequence is left to the competitor, the movements themselves are prescribed, as is the time allotted. The sequence of movements depends upon the horse and is chosen by the rider, and so constructed to show off the brilliance of the horse. Catherine likes to enter the rectangle at a "*galop rassemblé*". It is, she says, also better to do an "*appuyer au galop*" at first and end with a *piaffer* and a passage.

In the Musical Kür, if time permits, and if the horse is more powerful and his movements are more ample, the competitor can add some of his or her own flourishes, that is, the rider can embroider, can be imaginative. He or she can execute, as Catherine does, for example, alternatively, head and croup to the wall, or can execute successive half passes. But the choreography must at all times occupy the entire rectangle, never remain at one end.

Catherine on Spartacus at Versailles

With Orphée Catherine was never able to embroider and go beyond the required movements. Since the Trahkener is faster and his movements are more ample, she can use her imagination and go beyond the prescribed movements.

But Catherine was able to embroider when in 1998 French television asked her to simulate a bet made to the Marquis de la Bigne, a soldier and *écuyer* of distinction. Legend has it that the Marquis de la Bigne was asked to traverse the Place d'Armes at Versailles at a gallop in no more and no less than one hour. The length of the Place d'Armes is one hundred meters. It seems that Bigne accepted the bet and accomplished the "*galop*" by galloping in place, or rather, by advancing five cm by five cm at a time.

???XV, with wig and tricorne, Catherine galloped in place on Spartacus. Neither she nor the television crew wanted to tire her horse, so Catherine did the "stationary gallop" in short filmed increments. However, viewers of television had the impression that she had galloped the one hour in place, moving five cm by five cm.

During a conference of the Association pour l'Académie d'Art Equestre de Versailles, Catherine, riding Spartacus, in front of the Galerie des Glaces, and in the prescribed dress and music of the Grand Prix, executed the movements of *haute école*.

The Henriquets are established in Autouillet, about forty km from Paris. The farm goes back to 1556. There is a central courtyard which includes a large house in which they live, two L-shaped, one story buildings that contain stalls capable of housing about forty horses. There are two outside rectangles and one indoor *manège* with mirrors, skylights, and a small glassed-in gallery for the spectators. The 26 hectar area contains fields and woods. One two story building surrounding the courtyard has at the top about twenty little oval-shaped niches. I was intrigued by their function. It was in the late afternoon that I realized what they were used for: a roosting place for the many pigeons.

The establishment is, indeed, international in spirit. Pupils from many countries come to visit the Henriquets and receive lessons from both of them. Recently trainer, teacher, and writer, Pat Parelli, with his wife, visited the Henriquets, surrounded by a flock of journalists and interpreters. They watched Catherine ride her Trakehner and execute *haute école* movements. Pat Parelli was then asked if he or his wife wanted to ride. Another horse was brought in. Parelli first worked the horse in hand, then his wife rode, executing some *haute école* movements. Catherine continued to exercise her horse. Then Pat Parelli, removing the saddle, got on the horse. He retained the bridle but used the reins loosely. Some of us were surprised to see an American "cowboy," mustache and big hat, handling and riding an unknown horse with such gentleness and lightness, doing all the *haute école* movements with great finesse. It was, indeed, a revelation.

Thus to the inhabitants of Autouillet, the proprietors of the Fief de la Pannetière may have changed, but there remain certain remnants of the past. The buildings have only been repainted and, where necessary, strengthened or rebuilt. Hay is now being grown on the twenty-six hectares farm. Horses come and go, pupils come and go, visitors, well-known and unknown, come and go, but the Henriquets continue to train horses, and now even breed horses on the premises, attending to them all with loving care and understanding, and continue to teach competent and incompetent pupils coming from the five continents.

Michel Henriquet continues to train horses, teach pupils, write books and articles, make arrangements for their travels with their competing horses, and entertain the visiting greats and not so greats. He is, by the way, also an excellent chef.

And Catherine continues to train horses, instruct pupils, supervise the staff, attend clinics, get her horses and herself ready to compete in the Grand Prix and other trials, and practice medicine. Such is the life of this extraordinary couple.

ELOISE SCHWARZ KING

Initially, Eloise King was a musician by training and profession. But she, too, got hooked on horses. She began riding ponies when she was nine years old. She was small, light, and fearless. (She is still small, light, and fearless). She rode hunter and jumper ponies until the age of fifteen, when she began riding in open jumping classes horses owned by Samuel Magid.

In 1963 she bought her first horse and showed him in her first recognized dressage show. She also got into fox hunting. At a hunt breakfast she sang, unaccompanied, a fox hunting song called "Tally Ho." Her husband, (she was then recently married) was surprised at her singing. "I didn't know you could do that," he later said to her. Since he was also a musician they decided to bill professionally as "Tracy and Eloise," performing traditional country and folk music, singing and playing a number of instruments.

Eloise then began to concentrate on dressage. Joe Vanero, a prominent New York horseman, owned school horses who were being trained in elementary dressage. She began to participate in dressage competition but soon realized that she was neither enjoying her riding nor the intensity of competition. She only enjoyed those days when she could ride freely in the countryside.

In 1972 at the end of a fourth level dressage test, Eloise, despondent and with a sense of defeat, walked out of the arena knowing that she had won the dressage test. She did not want to have to listen one more time to a judge telling her to shorten her reins, to compress her horse more firmly between legs, to use more leg, to give more impulsion. She trotted out of the arena, put her horse in the trailer and returned to her farm. Stopping at the pasture gate, she opened the trailer, let her horse out and watched him canter up the slope, and gallop off. That very same horse had just finished a dressage test, executing a four beat canter. She then turned out her other horses, watching them canter up the slope. They were beautiful to watch. But she knew that she would never again be involved in dressage, especially competitive dressage. She would go back to the hunters, to the race track, back to the free and forward movement.

In a photocopy of an extract from *Horse and Hound* discussing the Wembley Horse Show of 26 November 1966, which Eloise showed me several years ago, I could see what Eloise's problem with the judges was. This extract was entitled "What the Dressage Camera saw." It is a sort of Swiftian "Modest Proposal" where the author gives the impression that he knows very little about horsemanship, yet reveals much insight about the nature of the photograph and in the comments he makes. The photograph and comments center primarily around the way the reins are used by Nuno Oliveira and by a member of the Spanish Riding School of Vienna. What the camera saw was Oliveira and his use of loose reins, and the very taut use of reins on the part of the member of the Spanish Riding School. It is this distinction between two styles of riding and the admonishment of a judge demanding a taut rein and the compression of the horse between the legs, that brought about Eloise's decision never to compete again.

Fortunately for the riding world, the resolution which Eloise took that somber day in 1972 did not last long. She was hooked once again when she saw Nuno Oliveira ride at the Potomac Horse Center. She also watched some home movies of Oliveira's favorite pupil, Bettina Drummond, riding in Portugal. And so the Mestre resuscitated Eloise's interest in the old discipline. Working with Oliveira now enabled her to understand the true meaning of the word "dressage," namely, that it denotes the training of a horse, pure and simple, that its purpose is to enhance the natural paces of the horse, to make him supple, balanced, light, and happy, and that this training should be used in all equestrian disciplines.

Thus whenever Oliveira came to the United States, Eloise, together with her horses, went to work with him at the Potomac Horse Center. She rode her horses daily. She rode for days without Oliveira saying a word. People would wonder why she bothered to work with someone who seldom or never uttered a word. But Eloise knew better. It was useless to explain that there was such a thing as a silent communication, facial expression, eyes, that said a great deal, that "said everything," as she put it. "I always understood what he was telling me, when I was executing movements incorrectly or when I was doing them well. I did not need words."

After working regularly with Oliveira for almost four years in the United States, Eloise went to Portugal in 1976. By now she had become familiar with the way Oliveira worked his horses, how he executed those wonderful movements with grace and elegance, how, without force, he got the utmost out of them, and how he was able to enhance their beauty. "There is no such thing as pushing of horses forward with the legs or compressing the horse between the legs. The reins are never taut. All the movements are executed with calm. The rider takes the appropriate position and the horse falls calmly and willingly into the appropriate position. There is never any punishment."

Thus this earlier contact with Oliveira in the United States prepared Eloise for the pilgrimage to Avasada and the pattern of equestrian life there. And so her own pattern as a maverick was established. She returned to Avasada two more times.

To support herself in Portugal, she, and two members of her family (husband and son) formed a small band and made music at Oliveira's establishment, as well as traveling throughout Portugal, playing traditional American folk music. The three members of the band carried with them eleven different instruments: several guitars, a banjo, fiddles, a base, a Cajun accordion, and a triangle. Her son, Peter, who had never ridden before, watching Oliveira ride, decided that he, too, wanted to ride.

Eloise has not completely given up participating in pure Classical riding. Many of her early teachers were oriented in the Classical idiom, teachers such as Lillian Wittmack Roye, Debra Dows and the brothers Fritz and Albert Stecken. What she has abandoned is the world of competition, training for sport, or training pupils for either competition or sport.

What Eloise opted for was the field of entertainment. It is when she sees the enthusiasm and joy that people express when she and her horse entertain them, when she can reveal to them the beauty and accomplishments of her horse, even his joy. "It is then that I find real pleasure. There is no competition in what I do. It is the two of us, just my horse and me, accompanied by music, who try to give pleasure to others. I and my horse dress up for the occasion. I become a clown, as does my horse, or a witch, a gay *señorita*, even Uncle Sam, anything that catches my fancy. I make all the clothes for the horse and for myself."

Indeed, it is no accident that the Musical Kür has recently been introduced in international dressage competition. The spectator, that is, the uninitiated spectator, was often bored watching traditional dressage, whatever the level. And so music, dressing up, a human dancing with his or her horse, has given new life to many a boring event.

Eloise's shows vary depending upon the size of the area in which she has to perform, the level of training the particular horse has reached, and the audience.

When Eloise performs, say, for a group of lawyers in someone's yard, or perhaps for a pony club group or a senior citizens' organization, she educates the audience as much as entertains them. She and her horse appear in very correct, traditional attire. Often she rides sidesaddle, her habit dating back to the 1880s. The horse is impeccably groomed with mane and tail braided.

Eloise enters with an animated trot, usually on a horse who is over sixteen hands. After demonstrating the walk, trot, canter, she then does the passage as she moves closer to the audience. She and her horse come to a halt. She proceeds to explain the movements she has been and will be doing. She instills quite a bit of humor in her explanations. The audience then asks questions. She follows with more riding, executing an extended trot, the Spanish walk, and gallops backwards. She also includes a jump over a relatively low fence. She gallops to the audience, halts, and horse

Eloise King clowning on an Arabian doing a rear for children at a birthday party.

and rider bow to the audience. If the horse she is riding is able to do so, she will include a *levade*, then drop her whip, which the horse retrieves. When he places it into her hand, he receives a piece of sugar. As the audience applauds, horse and rider exit as they entered: with a fast trot.

If the area in which she has to perform is extensive, Eloise can be more imaginative. Her costume can be anything from Tinkerbell, a witch, Cruella de Ville, or even a bride. The horse will be appropriately costumed: he will be painted to resemble a fairy, painted with spots, wear a conical hat. Under these circumstances, she enters the arena with a passage, coming to a halt in the center, and bows. She goes into a rapid canter, waving to the audience. This allows her the time to gage the audience and quickly determine whether they want a great deal of galloping or two-track work and side-stepping, that is, flash or elegance. She never performs too long, aware of an old maxim: always leave the audience hungry for more.

The spectator's attention span is not very long, thus it be better to give the audience a "fast punch," educate a little, and always execute a flashy exit. Naturally, there is always an encore. If the audience is

Eloise King on an Arabian doing the piaffe.

receptive, she includes the Spanish walk, a pirouette at the canter, a halt, a backwards canter, a halt. Bows and backs out of the ring. Furthermore, "a good announcer can make or break a show" says Eloise.

Sometimes Eloise makes use of an Iberian horse or a Lippizaner. In this case, she uses a Portuguese bull-fighting saddle and wears the traditional costume and hat of the Portuguese bull-fighters. The horse is decked with ribbons of two colors, which are looped down along his braided mane and showing on both sides of his neck.

While almost all the horses of the Portuguese are trained to be very fast in order to face bulls, these horsemen are also familiar with *haute école* movements.

In fact, many of the movements horse and rider have to execute when facing a bull are very similar to those used in *haute école*. Likewise, many *haute école* movements are similar to the movements knights made in battles. It is at the start of an afternoon's festivities in the bull ring that the horsemen enter the ring and execute all the movements their horses are trained to do.

Wearing the traditional costume and hat, but without the attending Portuguese horsemen and bull, Eloise gallops into the ring, reins in one hand, waving to the crowds with the other. In the

Eloise executing the levade.

center she spins first to the right, then to the left. She circles along the edge of the ring executing a two-track canter. She then does the same movement in the other direction. Back in the center, she does a pirouette to the right, halts, then one to the left, halts. Then comes a passage around the twenty meter circle. Back to the center and a number of *levades*, placing her first in one direction, then in the other. In a circle she executes flying changes at two or three strides, and along the diagonal, lead changes at every stride. With a fast gallop around the ring she waves to the applause of the crowd. She halts, executes a backwards walk, then a Spanish walk. She and her horse end the performance with a bow and exit the ring at a fast trot, waving to the crowd.

While Eloise has worked with many teachers, she considers Nuno Oliveira to be the most important teacher in her equestrian life and feels so very lucky to have been allowed to work with him. In fact the Mestre is still very much alive, not only in the heart and mind of Eloise, but in the hearts and minds of many of those who have worked with him. Indeed, it is quite remarkable to note how many horsemen and horsewomen from several continents have made this pilgrimage to Avasada. To this day, Eloise can never take a stride on her horse without feeling the awesome presence of Nuno Oliveira. In Reflections of Equestrian Art, Nuno Oliveira has said: "It is rare to see a rider who is truly passionate about the horse and his training, taking a profound interest in dressage with self-abnegation, and making this extraordinarily subtle work one of the dominant motivations of his life."

Knowing Eloise King, one gets the impression that she has this passion, this self-abnegation and has made "this extraordinarily subtle work" a dominant motivation of her life.

GERALDINE KATHARINA KNIE

Géraldine Katharina Knie belongs to a famous circus dynasty. She is the seventh generation of this dynasty which was founded by Friedrich Knie, born in 1784, the son of the personal physician to the Empress Maria Theresa. Friedrich Knie studied medicine for a while, but his contact with circus riders and a short-lived infatuation with an itinerant circus artist, made him throw medicine by the wayside. While this initial infatuation was short-lived, his love for the circus remained intact and he continued to be a circus artist. The year 1803 marks the year when the name Knie formally became part of the circus world: he soon made a name for himself as a tightrope walker, touring Europe with his recently acquired wife, Antonia Stauffer. Their courtship was far from being a traditional one. When the father of Antonia realized that his daughter was in love with an itinerant circus artist, he summarily put her in a convent. But the young circus artist would not give up. One night, in true melodramatic fashion, with storm and all, he entered the convent and eloped with his beloved. They married, of course.

Tightrope walking remained for a number of generations one of the main acts of the Knie family. It was Nina Knie whose performance on the tight-rope became legendary towards the end of the nineteenth century. During the seventy-fifth anniversary of the Knie Circus in 1974, at a gala performance in Zurich, Géraldine Knie, in honor of her ancestor, Nina Knie, walked across the ring on a tightrope, holding an umbrella.

The Knie Circus has had its troubles and almost dissolved on a number of occasions due to family differences. But the marriage of Karl Knie and Anastasie Maria Stauding in 1880 brought security to the Knie dynasty in that they had seven children who remained firmly within the circus. Berne eventually became the home base. Once again marriages and many offspring contributed to the continuation of the dynasty. It was in 1919 that four of the five Knie brothers formed the Swiss National Circus. It was during that same year that the decision was made to hold performances in a tent rather than in the open air. The marriage of Friederich Knie to Margrit Lippuner saw the birth of Fredy Knie Sr. and Rodolphe Knie. Today, the circus is in the hands of the son of Fredy Knie Sr., Fredy Knie Jr., and Franco Knie, son of Rodolpho (Rolf) Knie, who retired from the circus where he had served as clown and animal trainer to devote himself exclusively to the arts as actor and painter. For a while, Louis Knie was a member of the directorship, but he left in order to take over the Austrian National Circus.

It should be emphasized that the Swiss National circus is completely in private hands and receives no government subsidies. The influence of Fredy Knie, Sr., is very much visible, not only with respect to its adherence to the Classical principles as delineated by Philip Astley in 1776, but in its attitude towards the treatment and training of animals. This becomes immediately obvious when one watches Fredy Knie Jr. and Géraldine Knie train their horses for several hours each morning. Gentleness, immediate gratification with carrots or pellets for work well done, frequent caresses. A great deal of talking to the horses is done during rehearsal and training, as well as during performances, for talking to horses, says Géraldine, is bonding with them and calming them should it be necessary. This is the way they proceed with all their animals. There is never a harsh word uttered if a horse gets out of the order he has to follow; simply a touch of the whip. When the horses are transported from one town to another, Géraldine actually goes to the railroad station, helps with the unloading, and leads them to the area where the circus has pitched its tent. She also helps with the loading of the horses. It is her very presence and by talking to them, that the horses become calmer.

During these rehearsals and training sessions, the public is always welcome. It was Fredy Knie, Sr. who, at the age of eighteen, decided to open up the circus door to the general public in the mornings. The public can come and go freely, but, as a safety measure, is asked not to sit in the first row. These sessions are usually attended by children with their parents, who are usually quiet and attentive to what is occurring in the ring.

Géraldine received her training from her father. Always used to horses and other animals since birth, it is impossible for her to actually remember when she first sat on a horse. It seems as though there never had been a beginning. With grandfather, father, and mother on horses, surrounded by horses and other animals, in an atmosphere of travel and living in a caravan for about nine months, the world and atmosphere of the circus was the only logical one she could envisage and choose, that is, follow in the footsteps of her family. And Géraldine is quick to remind one that she had never been forced by her parents to chose this life and emphasizes to one and all that she cannot imagine any other kind of life. She says that she is very lucky that her private life and her professional life can blend so easily. As a teenager, her schooling for much of the time, depended upon tutors; when they were in Rapperswil, their home base and the circus' winter quarters, she attended regular school.

This passion and self-abnegation of which Nuno Oliveira has spoken and which Eloise King possesses, is also very much evident when one hears Géraldine speak of her work in the circus, her family, her horses. She began to work in the ring when she was about four years old. But she remembers more vividly the act of being removed from the back of the horse and that she began to cry. Although she had been performing on and off in the ring since age five, it was in 1989, at the age of sixteen, that Géraldine began to solo in *haute école*. At that time, her favorite horse was a Lusitano named Mogador.

Both father and daughter train the horses themselves, believing that by doing so they contribute to a better relationship with the horses. They do this every morning.

The circus uses only stallions and a variety of breeds: there are the black Friesians, dappled grey Arabians, light brown Palominos from England with flowing straw-colored manes, Iberian horses, even the famous Alter Reals, and several Russian Akhal-Tekkes.

During the opening of the daily performances of the year 2000, Fredy Knie appeared in the ring on Bolero, an Alter Real, executing flying changes at one tempo. He then gave the audience a little background on the origins of the present-day Classical circus and how their circus was in keeping with those tenets as delineated by Philip Astley in 1770.

Bolero, one of Géraldine's favorite horses, born in 1988, and which both she and Fredy Knie, Jr. ride, was a gift from her grandfather for Géraldine's twentieth birthday. Géraldine likes especially Iberian horses, for she likes their generosity—("in fact," she said, "they are too generous")—and because their conformation is ideal for training them to perform *haute école* equitation.

In October 2000, in Lausanne, Géraldine appeared on a grey with her mother, Mary-José, also a famous *ecuyère*, who, appeared on foot and handled trained white doves. While Mary-José had the doves do fancy foot and wing work, Géraldine executed the Spanish walk and the passage, while holding a dove in her hand which she then released to settle on the ring Mary-José held over her head.

Géraldine also performed The Post or The Courier of Saint Petersburg during that same evening. She first began to perform this act in 1991 when she was barely twenty years old. She repeated this performance in 1993 at the International Festival of Monte Carlo and received the much coveted Silver Clown; that same year she repeated this act at the Cirque Roncelli, and at the Theatre Carre in Amsterdam in December 1994 where the Circus Knie spends a month, taking only horses with them.

The Post (also known as *The Royal Post* or *The Courier of Saint Petersburg*, which was created by Andrew Ducrowat Astley's

Géraldine-Katharina Knie executing the *Courier of Saint-Petersburg* straddling two Frisians.

Amphitheatre in London in 1827), was performed by Géraldine on two black Friesians. In the past Géraldine and her mother, Mary-José Knie, have performed this act as a double presentation, each rider straddling her own team of horses. It should be mentioned that Fredy Knie, Jr. is always in the center of the ring directing the courier horses during this act.

The Courier of Saint Petersburg is a very ambitious, exciting, and fast moving (at times dangerous) circus act, requiring very precise team work and timing, for each horse—there are anywhere from eight to sixteen—has to be sent off at the precise moment to gallop between the two horses and under the legs of the rider straddling them, with the rider quickly having to pick up the long rein tied near the horse's withers.

Géraldine told me that during rehearsals, on occasion one of the horses would move farther away from the other horse and she would quickly have to jump off to avoid falling between the two horses and coming under their hooves. This act has also been accomplished by *ecuyères* such as Katja Schumann of the Big Apple Circus and Maude Gruss of Alexis Gruss' Cirque à l'Ancienne. In fact, *The Courier of Saint-Petersburg* is frequently the closing number of the Gruss' Cirque à l'Ancienne, with Alexis Gruss standing in the center of the ring and his daughter Maud standing astride with sometimes fourteen to sixteen horses passing beneath her and moving forward in twos or threes.

As noted earlier, in 1993 Géraldine received the Silver Clown from the hands of Princess Caroline of Monte Carlo, not only for her presentation of the Post, but for her excellent performances in the circus in general. In December 1977, Fredy Knie Sr. received the Golden Clown from the hands of Prince Rainier III of Monaco, while in February 1996, Fredy Knie Jr. received the Golden Clown from the

Mary-José Knie straddling three Frisians.

hands of Prince Albert of Monaco.

Circus Knie varies its performances, depending upon the type of audience they anticipate. They begin working on the new *programme* for the following season while they are still involved with the current season. When I mentioned to Géraldine the fact that both her grandfather and father had, at some time, executed *haute école* movements as well as other equestrian acts without bridle or saddle, she said that was the next act she wanted to accomplish.

Géraldine, together with her father, has also executed movements that are very traditional.

Géraldine-Katharine Knie in classical attire, the horse is doing the reverence.

Dressed in Classical attire, with *haut-de-forme*, and Géraldine riding sidesaddle, they perform such acts as *Pas de deux* or, when Mary-José is also involved, it becomes a *Pas de Trois* or a Quadrille with another *écuyer* or *écuyer*e.

It is precisely then that the Knie family performs what is considered the purest traditional kind of horsemanship. They also perform what is known as "working in tandem," that is, a rider on horseback, leads a second horse with long reins. It is this kind of horsemanship that would have delighted Baron de Vaux. It is this kind of horsemanship that in all probabilities delights the purists.
Fredy Jr. is very proud of his daughter and considers her one of the most outstanding women trainers of horses.

On two occasions during the morning training sessions, it was fascinating to observe Fredy Knie, Jr., Géraldine, and three assistants, teach a horse to kneel on both knees. The horse wore padded hobbles with rings at the back of each hobble. On each side of the horse, a leather strap was passed through the rings attached to the surcingle,

Géraldine-Katharine Knie in classical attire, the horse is doing the reverence.

situated below the horse's withers. The strap was then passed through two more rings attached to the surcingle, situated under the belly of the horse, just behind the forelegs. The leather strap was then passed through the two rings attached to each of the hobbles.

An assistant stood on each side of the horse at shoulder level. Each assistant held one side of the horse's rein in one hand, the strap which leads to the horse's hobble in the other. The horse must not be able to move backwards nor jump forwards. The trainer (on one day it was Fredy Knie, Jr. on the other day it was Géraldine), who, whip in hand, stood a little to the left of the horse and gently taped the near foreleg with the whip. When the horse raised his leg, the assistant had to pull the strap firmly but not brusquely and the horse's leg was kept bent until the trainer asked the assistant to let the leg down. Then the other leg was tapped. This was done a few times. At one point when the horse reacted by immediately raising his leg when touched, the other leg was then quickly tapped. With this second leg raised, the horse then naturally dropped to his knees.

Mission accomplished. The straps were then immediately loosened. After this successful performance, Géraldine gave the horse his reward: a tidbit, caresses, and praise. Not only are horses Géraldine's passion. There is also a little Yorkshire terrier named Elle who shares her sumptuous caravan. Her parents, living in a nearby larger caravan, have two larger dogs. A reporter once asked Géraldine what annoyed her most in life. "Hypocrisy" was her immediate answer. For Géraldine likes people who are honest and open. Her other aversion is cruelty to animals. She simply cannot understand how people can be cruel to these innocent and helpless creatures who depend so much upon humans. That is why the family, beginning with Fredy Knie, Sr. are so concerned about how their animals are treated and trained: only with gentleness and with the hope that others will follow their example. It is for the humane treatment and preservation of animals that the Knie family introduced a children's zoo in Rapperswil. The circus also takes along on its nine months' tour through Switzerland a number of animals who do not necessarily perform. This part of the zoo is placed in the immediate vicinity of the tent. Children can visit, ride the elephants, and ponies are available for the children to ride. It was especially delightful to watch the elephants enjoying a dip in Lake Geneva. As one wanders about in the zoo, what immediately catches one's eye is the specially high trailer made for the giraffe. Even more amusing is when the giraffe is ridden around

Géraldine-Katharina Knie executing the courbette or cabrade.

the ring for a few laps during a performance by its trainer Sacha Houcke to the delight of all. (Sacha Houcke is also an accomplished *écuyer* who sometimes participates with the Knie family in equestrian performances such as the quadrille). When asked about eating meat, Géraldine replied: "How can I, working so closely with animals—we also have cows and pigs at Rapperswil—eat animals." Thus both she and her parents are strict vegetarians.

The Knie family believes that there are some animals who should never be asked to perform in the circus. The bear belongs to that category. Indeed, one always has in mind the poor lonely bear, tied to a chain, forced to perform, sometimes being attacked by a dog. On the other hand, says the Knie family, there is reason to believe that horses like to perform. If one treats a horse with love, kindness, and fairness, he enjoys performing. "If one gives them love, they return this love" says Fredy Knie Sr. And watching the family as they train the horses every morning, love is in abundance.

When one considers present-day forms of entertainment, one realizes that the circus is one of the few modes of entertainment that has retained an authenticity and a continuity with the past. Unlike much of today's entertainment (especially what is advertised as entertainment on television), which has a phony and artificial aspect, the circus, that is, the Classical circus with only one thirteen meter ring, possesses this authenticity. "After all," says Géraldine, "when it comes to entertainment, where else can one simultaneously see, hear, feel, and smell the very source of one's entertainment?" For Géraldine-Katharina Knie, the circus is undoubtedly her dream profession. She cannot envisage another kind of world.

KATJA SCHUMANN BINDER

Katja Schumann belongs to another famous circus family, founded in 1871 by Gotthold Schumann (1825-1908) the year he came to Copenhagen. His son, Max, who became a Danish citizen in 1887, took over the management of the circus, which, in 1891 established itself definitely in Denmark. The circus toured much of Europe. Circus Max Schumann, as it called itself, happened to find itself in Switzerland at the outbreak of World War I and performances were suspended. Max Schumann would have preferred to disband the entire company, but his three sons wanted to continue, and the Circus Max Schumann became the Gebrüder Schumann Cirkus. In 1916 the newly formed circus traveled to Copenhagen, returning to Copenhagen each summer until 1969. In 1921 Circus Schumann finally settled in Stockholm, Sweden, in the beautiful building of Djurgarden. With two of the Schumann brothers performing regularly during the winter season at the Bertram Mill's Circus in London with equestrian acts, a pattern was formed: winter performances in London, early Spring performances in Goteborg and Stockholm's Djurgården, and May and summer in Copenhagen.

The three sons of Max Schumann had made their debut as bareback riders already with the circus of their grandfather, Gotthold Schumann. An accident forced Willy Schumann to devote himself to the business management of the circus. Horse training thus became the activity of the two brothers, Ernst and Oscar. They soon became world renowned horse trainers. They also became famous as trainers of horses at liberty and performing *haute école* movements. Oscar's sons, Albert Jr. and Max Jr. both born during WWI, helped Ernst Schumann with the training and riding of horses.

A brief female participation in horseback riding within the Schumann Circus took place with Cecilie Schumann, but she left the family circus when she married Johnny Hayes, an English bareback rider. Thus it was only when brother Max married Vivi Mikkelsen, daughter of a Danish veterinarian in 1946 and Brother Albert married Paulina Rivel, that women participated in equestrian acts. Thanks to Paulina a very definite cachet was given to equestrian acts with her outstanding equestrian talent, her elegant, sometimes fanciful costumes, and her musical innovations. According to Alf Danielson, writing on the "Circus in Scandinavia," in Renevey's *Le Grand Livre du Cirque*, *haute école* acts were given a new theme each year, enhanced by the rider's costumes and Paulina's musical innovations, thus reforming *haute école* equitation. She also trained horses at liberty. After the deaths of several family members, Albert and his wife, Paulina, took over the Schumann Circus.

Unfortunately the couple was beset by problems when they no longer had access to the building in Stockholm. An attempt to revive the tradition of a circus under a big top, came to naught.

Regular connection with the Bertam Mill's circus ended in 1967. Furthermore, Copenhagen's circus building had been sold to the future owners of a department store, who demanded an exorbitant rent. Adding to all these problems, public attendance was beginning to drop sharply, reaching the point that the profits did not even contribute to the care and feeding of the horses. Their horses had to be sold. In 1969 the Schumann Circus rented some of the "liberty" trained horses of the Krone Circus which Max and his daughter Katja presented.

It was in the spring of 1976 that Max Schumann decided to reorganize the famous Cirkus Schumann under a big top, and with his wife, Vivi, his daughter, Katja, and his son, Philip, opened the Cirkus M. Schumann in April 1977. In 1992 Max Schumann brought his world-renowned horsemanship to the Big Apple Circus. Katja Schumann had already joined the Big Apple Circus in 1981.

When Katja Schumann and then her father, Max Schumann, began to perform at the Big Apple Circus, they found a circus in the Classical tradition, that is, in accordance with "what circus is meant to be," with the audience "not far from the action in the ring." It is here where Katja performs and where she serves as trainer of the circus horses.

The Big Apple Circus was founded in 1977 by Paul Binder and Michael Christensen, "two young men who juggled in Sheridan Park, Washington Square Park, and Central Park—two young men recently returned from a fairytale adventure in a French one-ring circus, the Nouveau Cirque de Paris..." These two young men wanted to start a circus in New York City, a very special kind of circus whose orientation was not only artistically excellent, but which also served the community.

And so, twenty-three years ago, in 1977, they decided to form a not-for-profit circus that was exclusively devoted to entertaining the

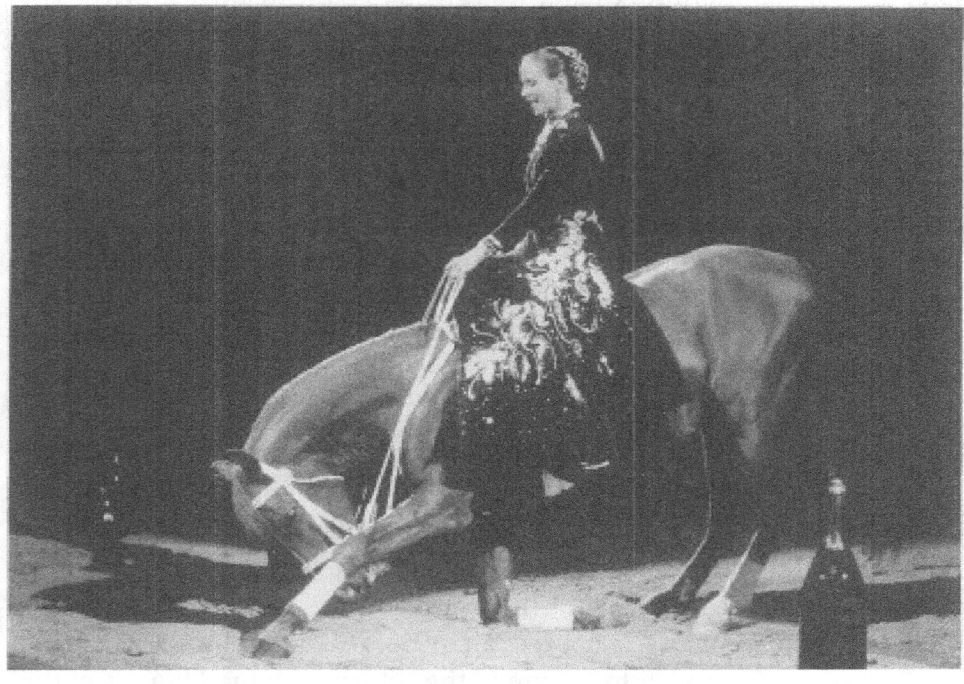

Katja Schumann on Khan doing the reverence.

family. Its aim was also to reach out and support several children's organizations by bringing joy to sight and hearing impaired children chronically and acutely ill children, and those in hospitals.

As is the case with circuses, present and past, the tone of the Big Apple Circus is international with respect to the performers they engage, as well as its permanent performers and staff, its artistic and creative directors and other permanent members of the group.

Every year the troop visits its thirty acre summer home, the Slifka Family Creative Center in Walden, NY, to rehearse the *programme* for the coming season. The circus' tour begins in Washington D.C., spends a few months at New York's Lincoln Center, and continues its tour in several eastern states. And yearly, Katja Schumann and her family and horses, follow the meanderings of this tour.

Katja made her debut in the circus world at the age of ten as a ballerina on horseback at the Cirkus Schumann in Copenhagen. But even without her famous background, Katja would have, indeed, established herself as *La Dame du Cirque* performing *haute école*, training and performing with horses at liberty, riding the baguette (a combination of an elongated hoop and a jumping rope which the rider swings over her head and then lowers to be in line with a rail, over which the horse jumps— timing is once again of the essence.)

Katja has also performed the "Courier of Saint Petersburg," the first woman to perform this act in the United States. She performed the "Courier" in 1986, not long after she joined the Big Apple Circus, and again in 1989/90. In the latter performance the production was entitled "Grandma goes West,"

Katja Schmann executing the baquette.

having a pony express motif, which included a message to "grandma." In an interview given in September 2000 to King Pole Katja said: "The message I was taking was written on a piece of parchment. At the end of the routine, I handed the message to 'grandma' and a recorded voice read it out. I changed the actual message on the parchment each day and 'grandma' and I had a lot of fun with private gags, trying to make 'grandma' laugh."

Executing the "Courier" was a considerable challenge to Katja as it was the first time she had performed it. Doing trick riding or bareback riding had not been part of her family's background; they did, instead, *haute école* or showed horses at liberty. But Katja was eager to do something different and challenging. Making the challenge even more complicated, the horse she was training to be her *haute école* horse and who at the time served as her outdoor horse, had not been trained to do trick riding. The routine itself was an additional challenge, since the people who had to send the horses into the ring at the correct time, had never been involved in this kind of work. But everyone, horses included, managed to sort things out and on opening night everything worked out well, timing and the necessary rapid tempo as well. The spectators gave the act a rousing applause.

In 1974 Katja won *La Dame du Cirque* award at the International Circus Festival of Monte Carlo. In 1976 she won the Gold Medal at the Circus World Championships in London.

Katja is married to Paul Binder, Founder and Artistic Director of The Big Apple Circus. They have two children, Katherine and Max. Both have appeared in a number of performances, with Katja and on their own. Katherine Schumann Binder made her debut in 1990 with "Ballerinas," "Horses and Clowns," and "The Golden Age"; her equestrian debut occurred in 1992 in "Goiri Places" with grandfather Max Schumann and mother Katja. Katherine is also an acrobat and performed in "Carnevale in Venice" in 1993 and soloed in "The Medicine Show" in 1996. During the 2000/2001 season she is performing in an aerial act entitled "Silk Aerial" with Sasha Nevidonski. Max Binder made his debut in "Goin' Places"[1] in 1992. His equestrian debut occurred in 1997 in "20 Years."

In a charming little book entitled Night after Night, the author, Diana Starr Cooper, tells us that Katja, *La Dame du Cirque*, while enchanting the spectators with her "equestrian wizardry... gave birth to her second child after performing in the evening show..." Indeed, the dictum 'the show must go on' is carried to its ultimate.

In this work, the author gives a detailed account of a night's attendance at The Big Apple Circus. The following is a description

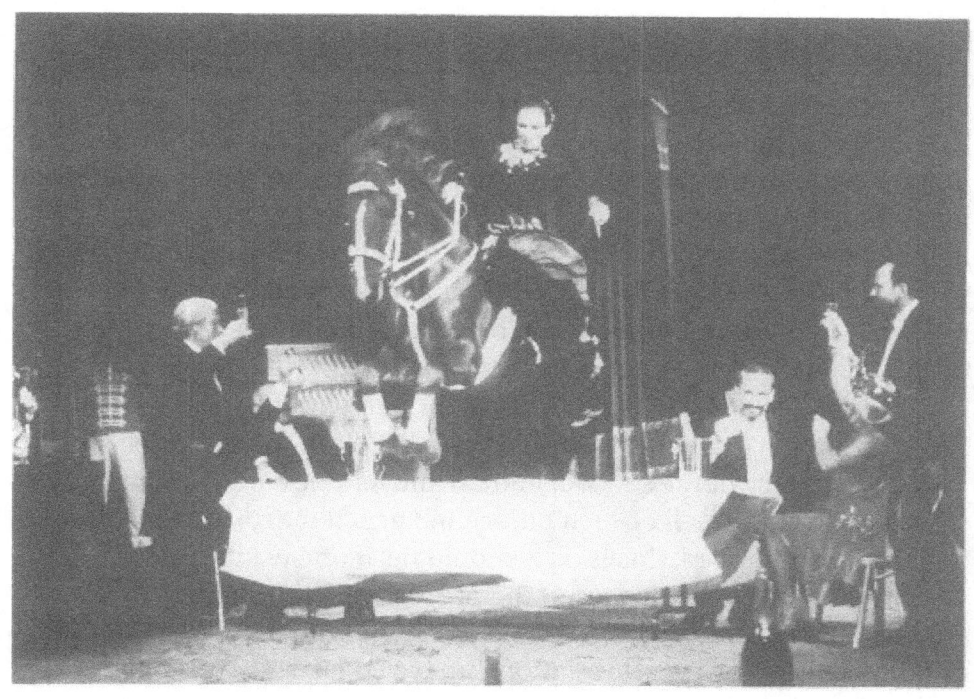

Katja Schumann jumping over the table.

of Katja Schumann which is completely in keeping with the photographs of Katja as seen in the yearly *programme* albums for a number of seasons. Cooper's account of Katja Schumann on this special night informs us that Katja is Scheherazade and that "we recognize her willowy bejeweled figure, her flowing hair and harem pants, and the clarity with which her vivid face and body express whatever she has in mind. But when she takes to the center of the ring, with her horses around her, the character and her genius suddenly make complete sense, Scheherazade is a horsewoman." Katja's act which Cooper experienced that night included six stallions at liberty "their free wills willingly engaged in hers."

    When Katja directs her horses, she quietly speaks to the horses, calling each one by name, her body moving in unison with that of the horses. "When she lifts her arms from her sides and steps forward, lifting her whole body up from the center, the stallions before her rise up rearing, balancing above her on their hind legs. They proceed to the edge of the ring, facing the audience, put their front hooves carefully on the ring curb, balancing there, necks arched, looming over the people in the first few rows in a stance of perfect stillness. Then, seemingly unbidden, called in a way that only they can comprehend, they fly off again."

The horses are decked "like mythic horses of the desert," putting the spectators in the mood of making them believe that they are in the midst of the world of Scheherazade.

Katja, like Géraldine, devotes each morning to the training of her horses for several hours. While at the Knie Circus there is much activity in the tent during the morning training sessions due to the attendance of many parents with their children, the tent of the Big Apple is empty, with only Katja and her horses in attendance. It is quiet. Only the trainer's "low, crooning voice" can be heard. But her body, moving quietly yet definitely, tells the horses what is expected of them.

Like Géraldine, Katja, also lives for and with her horses. Whether on the road or in portable stalls set close to her trailer, she is aware of every horse's move; human and equines are "in constant sight, sound, and smell of each other" and are "almost palpably attuned to each other." Indeed, this is as it should be, if one wants to work well with horses; it is "the essence of the process called training."

The relationship between Katja and her horses is free of force or domination. Nor is their relationship based on sentimentality. Rather, it is one of concern for the welfare of the horse, his needs, his requirements, which is primarily based on careful observation and logical and scientific thinking. Above all, it is with an atmosphere of calm, which Katja requires, that she can deal successfully with a horse and his training.

It is the policy of the Big Apple Circus for the trainers of performing animals to be always within reach of their partners. As is the case with Katja and her horses, the mobile homes of all the trainers are parked as close as possible to the housing of their partners.

The training of the circus animals is executed with patience and gentleness. Successful performance on the part of an animal partner always results in verbal praise, a caress or two, and a treat. As with the movements of *haute école* which are extensions of a horse's natural behavior and movement, the physical feats seen by the audience attending the circus "are actually extensions and refinements of gestures the animals exhibit naturally." The Big Apple Circus only focuses on animals who have "a traditional working relationship with man." Thus featured are the horse, the dog, and the elephant. Furthermore, the Big Apple Circus "never has, nor ever will, condone any form of animal abuse whatsoever."

GLOSSARY

Air(s)
Formalized movements of the horse. Low airs are those movements performed near the ground; they include the piaffe (*piaffer*), passage, volte, *gallopade*, change of hands, volte, *demi-volte*, pirouette. The high airs (*airs relevés*) apply to those movements when the horse springs from the ground to perform various movements such as the *levade*, courbette, *cabrade, croupade, ballotade, cabriole,* etc.

Amazone
Women who ride in the Bois de Boulogne for sport, attired in their elegant *amazone collant* [tights].

Ballotade
One of the high airs. A movement when the horse leaps into the air, legs all of the same height. He shows his heels as though he is about to kick, but does not throw them out.

Cabriole or *Capriole*
The horse leaves the ground. His hind legs are stretched out, front legs are bent. This is the most elevated of all the jumps.

Carrousel
A tilting match. Combat and parade exercises that replaced knightly tourneys. The most famous is the one that took place during the reign of Louis XIV, 20 June 1662, near the Tuileries in Paris. (Now known as the Place du Carrousel). The horsemen were divided into quadrilles, symbolizing various nations involved in sham combat. Today the *écuyer*s of the Spanish School of Vienna and the Ecole de Cavalerie of Saumur present their school exercises in the form of a *carrousel*.

Change of hands or leg changes or lead changes
One of the low airs. Action a horse makes with his legs when he changes lead. There are changes at every stride, at successive strides, at one, two, three, etc. *tempi*, flying changes. (In the past the fore legs were referred to as hands.)

Courbette
When a horse rises up in all his length, forelegs bent, hind legs extended). Also known as a *cabrade* (rearing). (See photo of Jenny de Rhaden and Blanche Allarty-Molier.) The *levade* describes a horse raising his forelegs off the ground while lowering his hocks. The horse does not rise up to his full-length as with the *courbette*. The horse must maintain his body for several seconds at an angle of forty-five degrees. When ridden, the *courbette* is often designed to confirm a

rider's seat. In the circus a horse does the *courbette* and jumps, hocks extended, forwards or backwards.

Courses de bagues et de têtes
Knightly games in use until the seventeenth century. The knight attempts to remove a ring dangling down with the point of his lance.

Demi-mondaine
Women who belong to the courtesan class, slightly shady, who do not belong to the *mondaines* (women of the world—upper class). Proust's protagonist, Swann, was infatuated with Odette de Crécy, a *demi-mondaine*. Another term for those shady ladies is *les horizontales.* On the opening night of the Cirque Molier, the *demi-mondaines* and the *horizontales de marques* were invited together with Le Tout-Paris.

Dressage, Dresser
In equestrian language, dressage means the training or education of a horse to the different gaits, exercises, transitions, etc. regardless of the discipline to which he will be put. The horse will also be trained to movements such as the volte, shoulder in, haunches in, half halt, etc. to flex and supple a horse's muscles, joints, etc., (*ressorts*), so that he will become resilient, collected, and light. Today, especially in the English speaking world, "dressage" means primarily movements executed by a "dressage horse" in competition.

Écuyer, Ecuyère
Horseman and horsewoman [respectively] who ride professionally, who ride in the circus, who teach in a riding school (*manège*), who train horses. The Ecole de Cavalerie at Saumur had an *Écuyer en Chef* and several *écuyers* to run the *Manège* des *Écuyers* in their capacity as teachers of future cavalrymen and other military men, and future teachers, as well as trainers of horses. A commandant ran the Ecole de Cavalerie.

Flexion
Putting the horse's flexor muscles into action—????certain muscular exercises contribute to the flexing and suppling of the horse's muscles, leading to *decontraction* [relaxation, removal of tension] (ex: volte, shoulder in).

Galop
Has been translated as canter. A canter usually describes a *petit galop* but can also mean a full gallop.

Haut-de-forme
A top hat usually worn by both the *écuyers* and *ecuyères*. By the *ecuyères* when attired in their *amazone* attire.

Hotel particulier
A private house or mansion in the city.

Lançade
This is movement when a horse makes a disciplined high bound or leap. Many purists objected to this movements as being too violent, but many *écuyer*s and *ecuyères* executed this movement.

Levade or *Pesade*
This movement is the introductory exercise to the high airs (*airs relevés*). (See *courbette*). Only the term, *pesade* was used centuries ago.

Panneau
A flat, oblong saddle, often used by the *écuyers* or *ecuyères* who vault or perform acrobatics on the horse, protecting them by making jumps softer as well as protecting the horse's back.

Passage
The passage is a very slow, very cadenced, and very elevated trot, swinging from one pair of diagonals to the other, with a period of suspension.

Piaffe or *Piaffer*
This is mobilisation of the horse's limbs, in diagonal pairs, without forward motion—the horse's mass is suspended between the beats of the diagonals. The *piaffe* is a passage in place and considerably more pronounced than the passage.

Quintaine, tilt at the *Quintaine* or *courir la Quintaine*
A common knightly sport during the Middle Ages, which consists in striking, by means of a lance, a revolving figure. If not performed skilfully the figure could swing around and strike the tilter.

Ramener
Flexion or yielding (relaxation) of the lower jaw which brings about the *ramener* at the poll, that is, collection which affects the head set or position. The *ramener* is an element that leads to the *rassembler*, that is, collection of the hindquarters, extending to all parts of the horse's body, affecting them all. The yielding of the jaw, the *ramener*, the *rassembler* bring about relaxation or *decontraction* (as opposed to contraction)—all contributing to that magical and desired state: a horse moving in lightness.

Rassembler
Collection is that state when the horse's haunches have achieved flexibility and are carried forward and under him—it is that state when the horse's equilibrium has reached its ideal stage. The

rassembler brings about the exact distribution of the horse's weight and strength between the forequarters and the hindquarters, supporting the horse's center of gravity. According to Maxime Gaussen, *écuyer* and writer on equitation, the *rassembler* is the basis for academic or *savante* equitation.

Relaxation or *decontraction*
This means an absence of sustained contraction; but never slacked muscles.

School Walk—*Pas d'école*
As opposed to a collected walk or a *pas rassemblé*. A very majestic, cadenced *haute école* walk. It is an ordinary walk, but perfected by movements that are more animated, more extended and higher than the ordinary walk. When the walk becomes diagonal, the horse will appear to be floating. It has little to do with the Spanish walk. In dressage competition, the *pas d'école* is considered a flaw. Only the collected walk and the extended walk is accepted.

Spanish Walk or Trot
A high stepping walk or trot that is cadenced and regular where the horse raises one foreleg at a time, propelling himself energetically with his hind legs. Not performed in dressage competition.

Le Tout-Paris
The upper crust, high society—those referred to as belonging to *le monde* (as opposed to the *demi-monde*).

Velocipede
Velocity propelled by one's feet. A bicycle.

Volte
A circle of six yards. The horse moves sideways on one or two tracks or treads, making two parallel circles. A very important exercise for flexing the horse's neck and shoulders. A volte reversed is the path described when the horse goes on two tracks with his head bent in the center. The forelegs describe a smaller inner circle, the hind legs a larger outer circle.

SELECTED BIBLIOGRAPHY

English writers tend to romanticize the circus, Americans to sensationalize it, only the French and one or two Germans have brought to bear on its involved technique a keen, critical faculty and treated it as an art quite as important in contemporary life as, for example, the ballet.
R. Toole-Stott, *Circus and Allied Arts.*

1. Adrian, Jacob Severe Russ, (Paul Adrian) *Histoire illustrée des cirques parisiens d'hier et d'aujourd'hui.* Bourg-la-Reine: Hauts-de-Seine, 1957.
2. Ibid., *Le Cirque commence à cheval*, Bourg-la-Reine: Hauts-de-Seine, 1968.
3. Cooper, Diana Starr, *Night After Night*, Washington, D.C.: Island Press, 1994.
4. Coxe, Antony Hippisley, *A Seat at the Circus*, London: Evans Bros., 1951.
5. Decarpentry, General, *Academic Equitation*, London: J.A. Allen, 1971. (Translated by Nicole Bartle).
6. Ibid., *Equitation académique*, Paris: Emile Hazan, 1972.
7. Disher, Willson, *The Greatest Show on Earth, As Performed for over a Century at Astley's (afterwards Sanger's) Royal Amphitheatre of Arts*, Westminster Bridge, London: G. Bell & Sons, 1937.
8. Etreillis, Baron d,' *Écuyers et Cavaliers autrefois et aujourd'hui*, Paris: L. Badoin, 1883.
9. Halperson, Josef von, *Das Buch vom Zirkus—Beiträge zur Geschichte der Wanderkünstlerwelt*, Duesseldorf: E. Lintz, 1926.
10. Holt, Richard, *Sport and Society in Modern France*, Hamden, Conn.: Archon Books, 1981.
11. Jando, Dominique, *Histoire mondiale du cirque*, Paris: Jean-Pierre Delarge, 1977.
12. Ibid., "When the Kirov was a Circus," *Le Cirque dans l'Univers*, 1997
13. Le Roux, Hughes, *Les Jeux du Cirque et la vie foraine*, Paris: E. Plon, 1898.
14. L'Hotte, Alexis-François, *Questions équestres*, Paris: E. Plon, 1906.
15. Ibid., *Un Officier de cavalerie—Souvenirs*, Paris: Plon-Nourrit, 1906.
16. Lijsen, H.J. and Sylvia Stanier, *Classical Circus Equitation*, London: J.A.Allen, 1993. (Translated by Antony Hippisley Coxe).
17. Molier, Ernest, *L'Equitation et le cheval,* Paris: Pierre Lafitte, 1911.
18. Rémy, Tristan, *La Belle Madame Lejars et ses soeurs Pauline et Armantine, Ecuyères romantiques.* Série "Documents," No. 11., 1960.
19. Renevey, Monica J. (ed), *Le Grand Livre du cirque*, 2 vols.

Geneve: Edito-Service, S.A., 1977.
20. Rhaden, Baronne Jenny de, *Le Roman de l'Ecuyère*, Paris: Charles Eitel, ed., 1902.
21. Saxon, A.H., *Enter Foot and Horse, A History of Hippodramas in England and France*, New Haven: Yale Univ. Press, 1978.
22. Seldes, Gilbert Vivian, *The Seven Lively Arts*, New York: Sagamore Press, 1957.
23. Signor Saltarino (Valdemar Otto), *Pauvres Saltimbanques*, Duesseldorf: Druck und Verlag Ed. Lintz, 1892 (in German, essays on famous circus personalities).
24. Thétard, Henry, *La Merveilleuse Histoire du cirque*, 2 vols., Paris: Prisma, 1947, Also Paris: Julliard, 1978.
25. Toole-Stott, R. *Circus and Allied Arts, A world bibliography*, 5 vols., Derby, England: Harpers & Sons, 1958, 1962, 1968.
26. Vaux, Baron de, *Écuyers et Ecuyères—Histoire des Cirques*, Paris: J. Rothschild, 1893.
27. Ibid., Les *Femmes de Sports*, Paris: C. Marpon et E. Flammarion, 1885.
28. Weber, Eugen, *My France—Politics*, Culture, Myth, Cambridge, Mass.: Harvard University Press, 1991.
29. Ibid., *France Fin de Siecle*, Cambridge, Mass.: The Belknap Press of Harvard Univ., 1986.

SELECTED BIBLIOGRAPHY OF BOOKS ON THE CIRCUS IN LITERATURE AND ART

1. Boll, Heinrich, *The Clown*
2. Bourget, Paul, *L'Ecuyère*
3. Champfleury, (Jules Husson), *Souvenirs des Funambules*
4. Colette, *L'Envers du Music Hall*
5. Daryl, Philippe, *La Petite Lambton*
6. Dickens, Charles, *Hard Times*
7. Ibid., *Memoires of Joseph Grimaldi*
8. Finney, Charles Grandison, *The Circus of Dr. Lao*
9. Gautier, Théophile, *Capitaine Fracasse*
10. Ibid., *Souvenirs de Theatre, d'Art et de Critique*
11. Goethe, Johann Wolfgang, *Wilhelm Meisters Lehrjahre*
12. Goncourt, Edmond de, *Les Frères Zemganno*
13. Guitry, Sacha, *Souvenirs Si j'ai bonne mémoire—(15 gravures et 6 dessins)*
14 Hardy, Thomas, *Human Shows, Far Fantasies, Soup and Trifles*
15. Herview, Louise, *L'Ame du cirque*—Essays
16. Holtei, Karl von, *Die Vagabunden*
17. Laing, Jan, *The Belle in the Top Hat*
18. Mac-Orlan, Pierre, *Aux Lumières de Paris*—Essays
19. Maeterlinck, Mauriac, *l'Hôte inconnu*—An essay on the Elberfeld horses
20. Mann, Thomas, *Confessions of Felix Krull*—Contains a desription of a circus in Paris
21. Miller, Henry, *The Smile at the Foot of the Ladder*
22. Montaigne, Michel de, *Essays*—Riding feats seen by the author while in Rome
23. Priestly, J.B., *At the Circus*
24. Proud'hon, P.-T., *P.-J. Proud'hon et l'Ecuyère de l'Hippodrome*
25. Queneau, Raymond, *Pierrot*
26. Ramuz, C.F., *Le Cirque*
27. Stanislavsky, Konstantin Alekseevich, *My Life in Art*, Ch. 5 "Playdays" (on the circus)
28. Thackery, William Makepeace, *The Newcomes*
29. Buffet, Bernard, *Mon Cirque* (19 plates, 6 in color)
30. Chagall, Marc, *Le Cirque* (lithos)
31. Degas, Edgar, *Mlle Lola* (painting of a circus artist—original is in the Tate Gallery, London)
31. Léger, Fernand, *Cirque* (30 lithos, text by the artist)
32. Renoir, Pierre August, *Two Little Circus Girls in the ring at the Medrano*, (hanging at the Art Institute of Chicago)
33. Rouault, George, *Le Cirque de l'Etoile filante* (Col. etchings and wood engravings of the circus)

34. Seurat, Georges, *Le Cirque, Banquistes,* and *La Parade* with 24 reproductions
35. Toulouse-Lautrec, Count Henri Marie Raymond de, *Au Cirque,* (39 plates of drawings in color of circus personalities)

ABOUT THIS BOOK

THE GREAT HORSEWOMEN OF THE 19TH CENTURY IN THE CIRCUS and an Epilogue on Four Contemporary Écuyeres: Catherine Durand Henriquet, Eloise Schwarz King, Géraldine Katharina Knie, and Katja Schumann Binder is a re-edition of *THE ECUYERE OF THE NINETEENTH CENTURY IN THE CIRCUS with an Epilogue on Four Contemporary Écuyeres, 2001.*

"Circus was quite a serious thing in nineteenth and early twentieth century Europe. Edmond and Jules de Goncourt noted in their Journal "We go to only one theater--the Circus. There we see clowns, tumblers....there is no false exhibition of talent..." Balzac believed that a circus equestrienne was worth more respect than an actress, a prima ballerina or an opera prima donna. And indeed, equestrians were the kings of the circus--and equestriennes, its idolized queens. For horsemanship was important then. It was more than mere entertainment. Wars had been won by good horsemen. Horses were still man's most valuable partner in so many aspects of everyday life.

And the circus had been created by and for equestrians...Nelson takes us to a wonderful, often surprising journey with the greatest circus equestriennes of the nineteenth century, who reigned with so much flair over the most prestigious rings of Europe...puts back the spotlight on these unjustly forgotten stars of the circus of yore...' Many of the moves illustrated are very familiar 'haute ecole' moves in classical dressage--piaffe, Spanish walk, passage; as well as the more esoteric 'airs above of the ground' most familiar today as performed by the Spanish Riding School in Vienna and the Cadre Noir in Saumur. These moves include the courbette, capriole, levade, pesade, etc. And these circuses were housed in grand, theatrical palaces, not movable tents; but in buildings as exquisite as the equestrians/equestriennes and their horses, a fitting setting for these memorable equine artists. Includes an extensive glossary.

The book is further enhanced by an Epilogue containing an account of the equestrian accomplishments of four contemporary écuyeres: Catherine Durand Henriquet, Eloise Schwarz King, Géraldine Katharina Knie, and Katja Schumann Binder.

www.ingramcontent.com/pod-product-compliance
Lightning Source LLC
Chambersburg PA
CBHW060513300426
44112CB00017B/2648